CHANGE IN THE CHURCH:
A SOURCE OF HOPE

BOOKS BY ROBERT C. WORLEY
Published by The Westminster Press

Change in the Church:
A Source of Hope

Preaching and Teaching
in the Earliest Church

Change in the Church: A Source of Hope

by
ROBERT C. WORLEY

THE WESTMINSTER PRESS

Philadelphia

Copyright © MCMLXXI The Westminster Press

Scripture quotations from the Revised Standard Version of the Bible are copyright, 1946 and 1952, by the Division of Christian Education of the National Council of Churches, and are used by permission.

ISBN 0–664–24901–9

LIBRARY OF CONGRESS CATALOG CARD No. 78–126354

Published by The Westminster Press®
Philadelphia, Pennsylvania

PRINTED IN THE UNITED STATES OF AMERICA

The Reverend Calvin DeVries, a churchman
and
my wife, Irene, a churchwoman

CONTENTS

The reason why Christian hope raises the "question of meaning" in an institutionalized life is, that in fact it cannot put up with these relationships. . . . It is in fact in a search of "other institutions," because it must expect true, eternal life, the true and eternal dignity of man, true and just relationships, from the coming kingdom of God. It will therefore endeavour to lead our modern institutions away from their own immanent tendency towards stabilization, will . . . open them to that elasticity which is demanded by openness towards the future for which it hopes.

—Jürgen Moltmann, *The Theology of Hope*

PREFACE

This book is written for the church, for laymen and ministers who need a statement around which they can discuss their expectations for the church and their concerns about the church. It is not intended to provide definitive answers, but to suggest ideas and directions for mutual reflection and action. We do not need debate so much as we need people openly discussing their ideas and commitments, and searching together for more mutually satisfying answers. Commitment to honest examination of both old and new ideas is essential. Awareness of the possibility of a more hopeful church, or at least a willingness to discover this possibility, ought to characterize those who read this book.

Ezra Stotland, in *The Psychology of Hope* (Jossey-Bass, Inc., 1969), has stated that "hopefulness is the necessary condition for action." Action as churchmen toward the church itself and as the church toward the world depends upon perception of the church as a hopeful organization. It is hopeful for its members and for the world as common, shared expectations develop. We are motivated to act as we perceive that our expectations have some possibility of fulfillment and that others recognize our concerns and become committed to act with us on them.

The reader should recognize the pluralism of expectations and concerns about the church and the world that can be found among us. Not all of these are consistent with Christian faith, but certainly most are, and many go unrecognized. The persons who have these unrecognized expectations and concerns do not find the church to be hopeful for them. Stotland, writing about the hope or lack of it in hospitals for the psychologically distressed, describes persons in the church as well: "People who are hopeless have been described as inactive, apathetic, dull. They feel, most simply, that there is no point in expending energy for no gain at all. Conversely, people who are hopeful are usually described as active, vigorous, energetic."

The basis for hope and action is the possibility that others can recognize our expectations and concerns and move with us toward them. In other words, hope does not reside solely in us. Hopefulness or hopelessness is to be found in every facet of church organizational life. In order for hopefulness to abound for laymen, clergy, women, children, and young people, we must examine this church of which we are a part.

We must look at it together, because no single individual is the basis for hope. *Together* we are both accountable and responsible for the hope of others. We create or destroy their basis for hope. Ruling groups of local churches, women's groups, renewal and restructure committees, classes for the education of church officers, and the variety of adult study groups should find new possibilities in church life while reading this book. Both clergy and laity should discuss together the issues raised and decide mutually on actions to be taken.

I am indebted to numerous people for many of the ideas stated here. Particularly I express gratitude to my colleagues on the McCormick Theological Seminary faculty, Jack L. Stotts, Thomas Parker, John Burkhart, and Ted Campbell. They will recognize both their influence and ideas.

Gratitude is also expressed to the Board of Directors of McCormick Seminary for the sabbatical leave that provided the time to write this book.

Dale Lake of New York State University of Albany, Robert Chin of Boston University, and L. Irving Pollitt will discover their influence on my thought. Eli Wismer of the Department of Educational Development, National Council of Churches, has encouraged me and allowed me to act upon my concern for more appropriate education of church leaders through the Organizational Change Project, which is sponsored by his department. The results of this project will be published.

Patti Houck has been most helpful in editing the manuscript so that it is both shorter and, hopefully, more readable. Mrs. Paul Hansen and Deanette Small exhibited amazing patience and skill in reading my handwritten copy to produce a typed manuscript.

My wife, Irene, and my children have lived through this book. It is important to note this, because the ideas found in the latter chapters have been verified by experience. My work with local congregations, middle judicatories, and national program agencies has taken me away from home too much. It has been essential to me to validate these ideas, to attempt to discover whether, in fact, the church can become more hopeful to itself and to the world. I am grateful to my family for their understanding and patience with a husband and father whose curiosity had to be satisfied.

R. C. W.

McCormick Seminary
Chicago, Illinois

1
RUGGED INDIVIDUALS—
OR CHURCHMEN?

Too long we have avoided, in theory and practice, an honest, straightforward attempt to think and act
as churchmen within the church.

Theologians since Karl Barth have done a great service
in bringing Christians once again to an understanding of
the Biblical and traditional ideas about the church. We
have been through discussions on the invisible and visible
church, the real church (as opposed to the existing unreal
church), the mystical body of Christ, the people of God,
community, koinonia, and so forth.

But thoughtful ministers and laymen have seldom understood how these discussions have anything concrete
and relevant to do with the church. They know an hon-
est-to-God sociological entity that has worship services,
committees, women's groups, men's organizations, educational programs, youth groups, and problems. Little help
has been given ministers and laymen in translating particular interpretations of Christian faith from abstract
theological expressions to functional, pertinent bases for
thought and action within church organizations.

Neither laity nor ministers have been prepared for

churchmanship. Theological seminaries have completely ignored the organizational structure of the church in their preparation of ministers. They blindly pursue their unreflective course of producing individuals for individual ministries in a complex, dynamic, organizational world. No seminary or denomination of which I am aware values the church or organizational ministry sufficiently to attempt to educate ministers as churchmen who can function effectively in church organizations.

The result is that most ministers are not churchmen. The anti-institutionalism of an increasing number of clergy attests to this. Those who are most anti-institutional gain their greatest satisfaction through radical individual activity. They interpret their life and work as the church in the world. The available alternative to the institutional church, as they view it, is (except in rare circumstances) only another kind of individual ministry.

The successful Protestant minister is one who excels in traditional, individual forms of ministry—preaching, teaching, and counseling. From them he derives most of his satisfactions, positive evaluations, and future securities. The underlying assumption is that the minister, as an individual, attempts to change men so they, as individuals, will do good in the world, and the layman enters into the picture because he shares this understanding of the nature of the ministry. There are few definitions of what it means to be a churchman and a minister. There are even fewer rewards for the minister who *is* a churchman, rather than one who gains reputation and reward for his own peculiar brand of individualism.

Ministers are hired on the basis of how well they change individual minds through preaching. The greatest preacher is the one who can find illustrations, who can turn words into more or less profound sentences and phrases, who can convince people through speaking that Christianity is good for them. The church's systems of reward and punishment are built upon individual accomplishments, or lack of them.

But these systems are disruptive of the common life and common good of the church. They encourage competition and conflict between ministers and laity and between ministers and ministers. Rugged individualism has been and continues to be disastrous in the church. Only too often, churches presided over by exceptional pulpit craftsmen are sick. Staff are unhappy, laity in rebellion, and groups in conflict. The lid keeps trying to pop off, so the brewing mess is always under the tension of some person or some group trying to keep order in the church. The preacher is constantly under pressure to preach one more sermon that will bring peace.

Furthermore, many of these craftsmen—honest, talented, and competent as preachers, teachers, and counselors—are extremely unhappy men. Some have left the ministry. Others are giving it one more try. Still others have resigned themselves to their lot—no other doors are open to them. They seem unable to escape to the local Office of Economic Opportunity, a social-work position, or a job selling insurance.

Perhaps some of these men and women should "escape." Some do not belong in the ministry. Many of these ministers, however, are needed desperately by the institutional church. They are superior human beings with intelligence, commitments, and concerns that are vital for the church's future. But these ministers (and some of the laity) are discovering that more than traditional individual skills are needed in an institutional church. Theory to guide thought and action is vital. The church has to recognize that it needs organization men to direct its corporate structures.

At present, changes of consequence in most denominations are administered by the staffs of boards of Christian education, homeland ministries, national missions, and the various judicatory offices. But preparation for these ministries is woefully lacking. Boards and agencies of the church usually employ persons because of past unique individual skills in churches and judicatories rather than because of qualities more appropriate to effective institutional life. Once persons are engaged in staff ministries, continuing education is whimsical, haphazard, and often unrelated to the problems of institutional church life and effectiveness in institutional change.

Within many of these organizations there is the same strife, tension, and frustration found in the local church (or in any other organization of society that still is run on the basis of nineteenth-century individualistic theory and practice). Staff persons in these organizations bear the brunt of much criticism by laity and ministers in local churches, which is often related to their gross ineffectiveness in organizational relations. They are the chief promoters of institutional change, but lack the theory, skills, and theological sophistication necessary for changing the church. Their only resort is to sheer power politics. Other alternatives, theory and practice in changing organizations, remain unexplored. Therefore many of the most promising people in church organizations are handicapped because they lack a theory that is functional in organizational life, and because they lack that theory and those skills necessary for effective organizational functioning and change.

Our history, tradition, and Scriptures should inform us that the church in the past has struggled with its organizational problems. Paul, in particular, agonized over the way in which the young churches would be cared for, and how they would respond to an alien world. He wrote, in Corinthians, of the dependency of the parts upon other parts and upon the head, Jesus Christ, for this wholeness and health. For too long we have allowed the various "members"—individuals, local churches, judicatories, and church boards and agencies—to rush in all directions, duplicating functions, wasting resources, totally ignoring the needs, skills, and resources of the entire body. We have recognized that the world outside is judged and directed by Christian faith, but we have failed to recognize that concrete forms of the church itself—its laity movements, its committees, its various groups, its staffs, its congregations—likewise fall under the direction and judgment of Christian faith.

Organization men, churchmen, are needed who can help laity to become reflective about the church itself. Ministers and laity are needed who can work with an organization to change that organization, as well as the individuals within it. The church is the *whole* church, comprised of local churches, judicatories, boards and agencies. And this church needs churchmen, laity and ministers, who can change it into an institution that is an embodiment of Christian faith.

Ignorance of the nature and character of institutions has led us to form absurd conclusions about the church as institution. The church certainly has some features in common with all other human institutions. It also manifests some profound differences because of its own unique sources and history, but the fact remains that Christians are human beings who, like all other men, create institutions that interpret and express some of their interests and commitments. And the institutional church is a human creation that has a relation to transcendent sources.

Ministers and laity engaged in individual forms of ministry are seldom plagued by their institutional creations, or are even aware of them. But problems arise for us churchmen when we begin to examine our convictions and commitments in the light of the created form arising from them (i.e., the church). This is a new enterprise for most of us. We are not accustomed to asking how the institutional church is or is not an expression of Christian faith. We do not think of the church as something living, interpreting, expressing dynamically and interdependently the convictions and commitments of men in relation to other human institutions. But the church *is* such a living creation! It embodies the truths, interests, purposes, and commitments of its people through every thread of its life.

The task of ministers and laymen is to reflect critically as Christians about the truth or truths, the expressions of Christian faith, embodied in the institutional church, and then together, mutually and cooperatively, to change the institutional church until it approximates more closely a common understanding of Christian faith. Ministers and laity, as churchmen, should be agents of institutional change to the end that Christian faith is interpreted and expressed in every facet of the institutional church.

This point of view is a radical departure from the traditional Protestant understanding of the ministry, in which the people of the church are not self-conscious about the church itself or the ministry to this church, except as the church ministers to individuals. We are concerned here for some of those lost Biblical images which insist that the people, the church, the body of Christ, must care for itself as well as the world. In fact, it must care for itself in order that it may care for the world.

There has been too much anti-institutionalism, aimed against both the church and other human institutions, by those who do not ask what it will take to transform the church. There needs to be a general understanding of how the institutional church lives in the world, how it can maintain and transform itself, and what kind of ministers and laity are needed if the church is to be a source of hope in the world. The first step is to move beyond the rugged individualism of our immediate past to an understanding of the churchman as one who has a mandate to change the institutional church to where its very life is an expression of Christian faith in a complex, dynamic, interdependent, institutional world.

2

THE CHURCH AS A DYNAMIC, INTERDEPENDENT INSTITUTION

Our Western world is a world of complex, dynamic institutional life. People spend their lives participating in a variety of institutions, industrial, political, legal, leisure, family, and religious. In each of these institutions people learn attitudes, values, ideas, skills, and commitments. Although the methods of teaching vary remarkably from institution to institution, each is effective to some degree in its teaching and the teaching of each is interdependent on that of the others.

In a *stable* society various institutions can and do reinforce, supplement, and generally affirm the life spent in other institutions. Schools, churches, families, and local communities tend to agree with one another. Slavery, for example, was never merely a legal or political way of life. It was condoned by the church, accepted by familial society, and reinforced by an educational system that seldom provided for the children of slaves.

In an open, pluralistic, rapidly changing society, however, learning in one institution often contradicts, challenges, and denies the validity of learning in another institution. Conflicts, and indeed polarization, develop between families and schools, communities and schools, churches and communities, churches and schools, families and work institutions. Citizens of the middle class in the United States today, and most particularly members of the upper middle class, are experiencing intensely all the conflicts, contradictions, tensions, and frustrations of changing institutions. In this group, traditional values, traditional ways of solving problems, and traditional views of the world and man are most frequently challenged.

Every institution of the affluent upper middle class is being transformed. Family life, work life, play life, and educational life have all undergone dramatic changes since 1945. We have only to reflect on the changes in our own lives to understand something of the magnitude and rapidity of change. But change produces tension, frustration, and ambiguities.

Husbands and wives are redefining the meaning of marriage, parenthood, and family life. Young people and adults are developing new, cooperative styles of relations. The entire educational establishment—administrators, teachers, students, and school boards—is engaged in dramatic confrontation, and education itself is subjected to serious scrutiny in a society that is redefining the nature and role of schools in the preparation of all its citizens to participate in that society.

Maximum confusion and ambiguity surround our political and legal institutions. New coalitions arise in politics. Repeated attacks are made from all sides upon our legal institutions as the law is continuously reinterpreted under new conditions. Every institution, living interdependently, has to change, and in the process each must deal with the conditions, the processes, and the end results of changing.

Lest there be misunderstanding and even arrogance on our part, we need to recognize that these same institutions—family, educational, professional, leisure, political, and legal—have not been subject to so great and rapid change in the case of the poor segments of the population of this country and the world. On a worldwide basis, only a very few people live and participate in a dynamic, somewhat open, changing society.

But the poor, particularly the black poor, have begun a process of changing their own institutions—political, legal, educational, etc. The consequences for all are great, because transformations in the institutions of the poor will have effects on our institutions. During this current period of maximum confusion, suspicion, anxiety, and unrest, the question is not *whether* our common institutions will be affected, but *how* they will be affected.

Interdependency and interrelatedness are facts of human life. White institutions have consequences for black institutions, and the reverse is also true. We cannot change ourselves without changing others. Others cannot change without changing us. Across the world, even in the southern hemisphere where the poor predominate, the movement to change existing institutions, to take into account new conditions, new values, and new desires of men, is gathering momentum.

The church, even though it has a unique source of life, Jesus of Nazareth, is institutionally very much in this world. It experiences the changes and knows the tensions, ambiguities, and frustrations of living interdependently in a changing world. It has the same polarizations within

it that all other institutions of society have had to acknowledge.

Signs and symptoms are numerous. From local parish
to denominational boards and agencies, crisis follows
crisis. Laymen revolt, liberal and conservative withhold
their pledges and drop out. Some dissent and withdraw
because the church is not involved enough in social issues. Others withhold money and organize groups to protest because the church is *too* involved in social issues
and has lost its concern for the individual and the "spiritual."

The insecurity and anxiety of many men in the ministry is due much of the time to their inability to deal
satisfactorily with the alienated factions within the
church. Few ministers have the requisite knowledge and
skill to enable an organization to function during these
crises. Goodwill and good-intentions-with-a-dose-of-
piety, they have discovered, are not sufficient for solving
organizational problems involving the alienation and reconciliation of concerned groups.

Churches have employed multiple staffs in order that
specialization and compartmentalization will bring increased competency in particular areas. But often this
strategy has backfired. The problems of multiple staffs
are notorious, mainly because church staffs have not
learned to function in cooperative, nonpaternalistic, non-
competitive ways. Senior ministers, most of whom came
from the era of rugged individualism, have not been educated to maintain a healthy church where pluralism is appreciated, and where staff relations are such that the
contributions of each member are maximized. Only too
often staffs are controlled by a nineteenth-century board

of directors, with a leader-minister attempting to cope with problems of an institution that is decidedly in another world.

Many churches are characterized by their exclusiveness. The message for dissidents may be either explicit or implicit by minister and/or "directors": If you don't like the way we run this church, you can leave. These same ministers and laity manipulate elections in churches to minimize conflict and differences rather than openly dealing with their sources. Pluralism, rather than being a source of creativity, new energy, and fresh ideas, is looked upon as a source of trouble, and is, therefore, to be avoided. Aversion to dealing with differences is justified through the idea that such differences and conflict over these differences are unchristian. The Christian thing to do is to ignore differences and thereby make it impossible for people to be reconciled.

Because of internal turmoil, few churches are healthy enough to deal with the conflicting demands of a world outside that is also in turmoil. Many churches retreat from external challenges to form new expressions of monasticism, twentieth-century style—enclaves for the like-minded. Other churches simply adapt to the claims, values, and attitudes of the world, showing little ability either to reflect critically or to stand in a constructive relation to other institutions and the challenges presented by those institutions. Very few churches have the internal structures, the processes, and a theology with which they can meet the challenges of the external world with an integrity and appropriateness expressive of Christian faith. We have not learned that external stimuli—problems from the world outside—create internal problems that must be met by an internal organization designed to meet problems.

From local church to denominational board and agency, we are plagued with the legacy of an inadequate understanding of human organizations. It is as though we in the church had learned nothing about organizations, leadership, and maximization of human potential since Max Weber studied the Prussian Army and the Roman Catholic Church and wrote a description of them that still characterizes, all too frequently, our own church organizations.

Weber described a mechanical, hierarchical, impersonal organization in which every person had his niche. Innovation, initiation, and energy for responding to challenges came primarily from the top down through the echelons of workers, soldiers, and priests. People in the organizations he described seemed incapable of revolt, thwarted creativity, and felt the meaninglessness of their work or their position in the organization.

The church cannot cope with multiple challenges, internal and external, until it updates its understanding of organizations and leadership. At present, several new conditions are developing that mean death for previous understandings. These forces and ideas, and the commitments behind them, are at work in all the institutions of Western society, and they are affecting every aspect of church life, including the theological commitments of the people. As part of an interdependent, dynamic, institutional world, we may better understand ourselves as the church if we know what they are.

1. First, and perhaps foremost, knowledge of the world and of ourselves has become readily available. From

nursery school through never-ending "continuing education" (and certainly by the mass media), we are bombarded with psychological and sociological concepts, and our increasing perspectives on ourselves and our place in history lead us to reevaluate past formulas—sexual roles and mores, the value of work versus leisure, etc. Both personal and organizational life are continuously scrutinized. We probe for more depth in family life and work life, are no longer satisfied with perfunctory relationships, and in all phases of life have definite ideas of how we want to be treated as human beings.

2. At the same time, different life-styles are visible and in open competition with one another. To be a young businessman with tensions and ready cash, or a hippie with few worries and only the security of the commune? Or, for a churchman, to be a committeeman and try to affect structures, or to be an individualist, disregarding the structures and doing what good you can on your own? Participation in a variety of organizations gives us bases to judge and choose those organizations with life-styles that allow us to contribute what we can and that offer us the most satisfaction. We reject and withdraw our commitment and support from those organizations, including the church, that fail to fulfill or satisfy us.

3. As we become more knowledgeable and more aware of alternative life-styles, the *authority* of any single idea, pattern of life, or person is confronted and challenged. Authority is no longer static, but shifts rapidly according to situation. No person may claim authority merely by the position he holds—be he president, pope, personnel director, or preacher—for authority resides primarily in those who give it and for only as long as the givers con-

tinue to give it. A minister, for example, may have the formal authority to preach and conduct worship each Sunday, but nothing he says is authoritative for the people filling the pews. They decide for themselves if and when they will hear him.

Neither is historical precedent or tradition authoritative for most people. On occasion, particular groups and individuals decide to let some bit of history or tradition inform their thinking. But in contemporary organizations, whether industry, school, church, or family, fewer and fewer people will accept answers of the past without careful scrutiny. The faith of our fathers, the solutions of our fathers, and the methods of our fathers are as subject to criticism as any other sources of information. In fact, it is often fatal to mention that any solution, idea, or method had its origin in the past.

We are becoming a people who trust processes and structures rather than persons, ideas, or precedent. We may think that leaders are good people, but our trust of them and their ideas is greatly enhanced when the processes and structures of decision-making are such that we know that information, interests, and commitments important for us are included. This is the phenomenon of democratization that pervades all our organizations. It is being pursued in church organizations with the same relentless energy as in business, industry, schools, and families.

4. The problem of power is also universal in our society. It is not confined to the relations of black people or poor people to white middle-class institutions. It is a fundamental problem for most of the people participating in *all* our institutions.

To be powerful, to have power, means to be able to influence the decisions that affect you and others in a mutual process. Power resides in groups, in the dynamic relations between groups, and among particular people in these groups. These powerful people, in their time of power, control the processes taking place between people, the communication possible and probable, and, much of the time, the content of that communication. Other people in the institution never have access to power because they are structurally prohibited from participating in the decisions that affect their lives.

The church is no exception in our organizational world to the practice of institutionalizing power and powerlessness. Some people and groups within the church—for example, youth, women, racial minorities, nonofficer males —are deliberately or thoughtlessly kept off committees, deprived of information, and denied access to communication channels. Ministers and laymen have an abundance of religious rhetoric, but theological reflection on the ways in which love, power, and justice should prevail in the organizational life of the church is almost totally lacking.

5. Another force at work on Western institutions is the intensification and condensation of human experience through electronic mass media. Although this has primarily affected the young, it has consequences for all age groups and organizations. As we experience worldwide events with a high degree of intensity—assassinations, coronations, military combat, Olympic games—we develop styles by which we desire to experience the whole world. Gradual experiencing is becoming increasingly difficult. We do not want to delay experience until a later time. But this presents special problems to an institution such

as the church, accustomed to slower-paced modes of expression (committees and traditional worship and styles of education).

6. Hand in hand with intensification of experience goes a new complexity of language. Words convey particular meanings within the framework of particular groups of people and their relations with other groups at a given moment. No group can control entirely the meanings of the words it uses. Nor does it have power irrespective of other groups to use words with particular meanings as it may desire.

Yet in the church we have assumed a kind of linguistic imperialism in which words have a meaning and a power in themselves apart from social and cultural realities surrounding them. Now we must no longer assume that religious words carry meaning across complex organizational life. If religious language is to have universal meaning (and there is cause to question whether this is possible), then words must be found that have some degree of relevance in a variety of organizations.

The languages of the behavioral and social sciences may apply more extensively to our society than do any other languages at this moment. Just as does theology, these sciences deal with many of the basic issues of man's existence. In this book we shall explore the possibility of developing a relation between theology and the social sciences, particularly organizational theory, to see if appropriate terms can be found for reflecting about the church and its ministry.

All human organizations have been and continue to be affected by the six features of contemporary life just described. Basic transformations are being wrought in all organizations, including church organizations, and because they function interdependently the pressure to change is immense. It is important for church people to understand that the church is not alone in experiencing crises. The church is a microcosm of the world, with interdependent parts and concomitant problems, just as it is a part of the world of organizations—not some special, insulated, isolated institution. The church, just as every organization experiencing these realities, must deal with them either negatively, by denying them, or positively, by coping with them.

The future life or death of any organization is at stake in the decisions and practices that deal with these realities of contemporary life. The tendency toward death is as characteristic of human organizations as it is of physical-chemical systems described by the second law of thermodynamics. The attempt to retreat, to isolate oneself, to preserve the past in the face of multiple challenges, can only mean death for any organization.

Energy for continued life and health in an organization is not self-generating. Every living thing receives its energy, its food for life, outside itself. No living organism or organization is self-sufficient. Life depends not only on that which it receives quantitatively from external sources, but on what it receives qualitatively. Like a human organism, an organization can be purposeful in determining, at least to some degree, what it will receive and what it will do with what it receives. This can be called *purposeful interdependency*. We are not *just* interdependent, being influenced at will by the forces around us. Purpose, the purpose of the church, can bring a new dimension into our necessary, unavoidable relationships.

This phenomenon of *purposeful interdependency* introduces a hopeful note into church life. New sources of knowledge, the visibility of new and different patterns of life, changes in the nature of authority and power, the impact of electronic mass media, and our awareness of the nature, dynamism, and complexity of language mean new sources of energy are available to us. The church with a purpose, people called Christians with a purpose, can qualify, use, direct, and judge all these sources of energy to transform and sustain life in the church as an organization.

Democratization of the church means more people with commitments and interests available for ministry. Use of new sources of knowledge means greater self-understanding and more tools for translating and interpreting Christian faith. Realism about religious language and the languages around us means the possibility of increased communication of the meaning of Christian faith. To live interdependently, even with forces that at times seem destructive, means that we, in fact, have a source of hope, not fear.

3

THE CHARACTER OF THE CHURCH
AS ORGANIZATION

Langdon Gilkey, in his book *Shantung Compound*, describes two events in the lives of a group of people interned during World War II in China by the Japanese. Space was at a premium in the camp and particularly in the sleeping quarters. Nine to eleven persons were housed in a ten-by-eleven-foot room. Most of the people were Christian missionaries, Christian businessmen and their wives, teachers, and British government officials. It was impossible for these people to arrive at an equitable and just allotment of space. Good, educated, enlightened people who could tell others what Christianity was about, and who were products of Christianity themselves, could not and did not implement that faith in living as a social group in an institutional arrangement.

At one point the American Red Cross sent fifteen hundred parcels of food to the camp. The Japanese in permitting the packages to be sent into the camp suggested that one and a half parcels be given to every American prisoner and that one parcel be given to all other prisoners. The majority of Americans wanted all seven and a half parcels, which was their share if none were given to others, to do with as they pleased. In both instances, as in most other problem times, the character of the camp was such that the problems were solved only by recourse to the power and authority of the Japanese captors.

Gilkey concluded this section of his reflections with the words: "I am sure that Christian moralists ought to be as much concerned with the character of their social structures as with the problems of personal goodness: here is precisely where we find it most intensely difficult to be just and generous."

The idea that social structures have a character ought not to be difficult to understand. Every family has a character that is revealed in the relations between parents and children, the way in which decisions are made, and the experiences parents deem important for the development of children into particular kinds of mature, thoughtful adults. We see something of this dominant character when we examine the overarching values, interests, and commitments of family members. Some parents work hard at creating and maintaining a particular character to their family life. Others take family character for granted and duplicate, to a great extent, the character of their own childhood family life. Still others have no concern, and the character of their family life is determined inadvertently out of the multiple experiences and activities of life.

The church is no exception to this observation. Local churches, church organizations of all kinds, including boards and agencies, have a character. Church schools and church school classes have a character. Every group or organization has expectancies, norms, values, interests, ways of resolving differences, leadership patterns, and activities that are the concrete expressions of its character. Character consists of more than the structure of an organization. Structure, and the limits imposed upon people, tasks, and goals by structure, is only one aspect of organizational life. It is the total organization in its dynamic, expressive complexity that has profound effect upon people.

Within the overall character of a church organization are the thinking and acting behaviors of ministers and laity, which are for the most part consistent with the character of the organization. In the past, little thought has been given to the character of the institutional church and how this character might be transformed to interpret and express Christian faith more effectively. We have little understanding of what a transformation of this character in an interdependent, institutional world means for the ministry of laity and clergy. Let us turn now to seek an understanding of the character or personality of the institutional church.

Some churches exist as a dull, closed, apathetic people who have not mobilized the available potential energy of people for study, thinking, and action. Still other churches and church organizations are best described as polarized groups in which no group hears, sees, or understands any point of view other than its own. In these organizations more time is spent defending claims of correctness and purity of Christian viewpoint, appropriateness of strategy, or adequacy of ideas and materials than in attempting to discern what it means to be the body of Christ in which there is reconciliation, pluralism of function and perspective, and mutuality.

Other churches and church organizations are run like a

"tight ship," with the minister or administrator and a very small group of people making all the decisions, controlling communication, and maintaining their own theological, social, and economic interests.

But some churches and church organizations are open to new ideas, flexible, free to meet a variety of challenges, innovative, and able to value and use the contributions of *all* members. These churches can be characterized as a people who are engaged in free and lively study and discussion with open disagreement *and* reconciliation.

Too frequently we focus upon the mission of the church to the world without realizing that the church is the world in microcosm, and that perhaps there is need for mission to the church. The same alienation, anxiety, injustice, and lack of respect that characterize the world also characterize many church organizations.

Our emphasis on the world as the mission field of the church may have allowed ministers and laymen to escape too easily from carefully scrutinizing the church itself. In a dynamic, interdependent, rapidly changing world the line that is drawn between church and world is misleading. Churchmen are in both church organizations and the world. When they are in church organizations there is no escaping the effects of the world. In this microcosm of the world, the church, a universal method of reflection and action toward both the church and the world may be developed.

There are, as has been claimed, universal similarities between church and world. If laymen and ministers can think as Christians and act to implement Christian theology in church organizations, there is hope for the world. If alienation, mistrust, polarization, and injustice cannot be dealt with in church organizations by churchmen, there is little hope that churchmen will be able to deal with universal realities in the world.

Churchmen, both ministers and laymen, are given the church to transform into a living, visible expression of Christian faith. The church is the object of our commitments and energy, not for itself, its salvation, or its success, but because the church has the world as its object. The church lives for the sake of the world.

We have been developing an understanding of the church organization as something more than a collection of individuals gathered together around a leader who exhorts them to engage in Christian activities directed toward the world, or as a collection of individuals gathered in a church bureaucracy for appointed tasks aimed toward some organizational goals. The church as an organization is a collective entity that has a personality, character, or climate of its own. The character or climate of that organization influences to a great degree the commitment people give to the church and what they actually *receive, hear,* and *understand* of the church's faith, life, and message. The church organization as organization teaches.

One way to understand this concept may be to think of the church organization as a massive amount of information that is stored, as in a supermarket. This analogy does not refer merely to the church library, Christian education program, or other resources we commonly lump under the term "information." Information is stored in the architecture and in fact in all the physical shapes and characteristics that surround the living organization as it gathers. Information is available in all the activities of the minister—Sunday worship services are only one source of information. Information is also available in the work of the pastor as preacher-teacher and counselor. Formal committee meetings and congregational meetings are rich stores of information. Even more important is the information available in informal relationships and activities.

It is not difficult to appreciate the amount of information confronting people through the formal tasks, goals, functioning, and decisions of church organization committees. It is more difficult to appreciate the concept of stored information in the *styles of leadership* of ministers and laymen. It is most difficult to recognize that a massive amount of information is ready to be shared with those who experience the *character or climate* of an organization. *Every aspect of the church organization is information available to participative persons.*

Some may object to thinking of the church as information. Or they may readily see the church as cultural, but have difficulty in comprehending the information concept. To place the development of information theory in perspective, Otis Duncan cites a comment of I. H. Siebel: "'Information' . . . is increasingly being recognized as a fundamental economic and technological 'stuff' comparable to matter and energy." Duncan suggests that "today's effort to generalize the information concept is perhaps no more radical for its time than were the hypotheses of energy conservation and interconvertibility of forms of energy a little more than a century ago." (Otis D. Duncan, "Social Organization and the Eco System," in *Handbook of Modern Sociology*, ed. by Robert E. L. Faris, p. 40; Rand McNally & Company, 1964.)

Another way of putting it is that the concept of information pushes us beyond the old debates in which we placed culture against society and argued which was more powerful in shaping human behavior, or in which we tried to arrange artifacts along the lines of culture or society. The idea of an organizational character suggests that information is available in organizations elsewhere than at the formal sources of messages. The *total church* is an alive, teeming source of information.

The problem for the church, as for all human organizations, is the nature of the information available. What is to qualify, to judge, to inform, to direct the thoughts and actions of men in the creation of information? How do theological commitments come to bear upon the creation of information? To pose the question in another manner, How do theological commitments guide, direct, and judge the maintenance, support, and change of church organizations? If all organizational life is information, is some information a more proximate expression of Christian faith than other information?

The concept of the church organization as a source of information, conceived in the broadest terms possible, creates the possibility of a thoughtfulness about church life not possible before such conceptual and practical aid. When every facet of church organizational life is understood as information for others and ourselves, then the task is before us to decide the nature, quality, direction, and timing of that information.

We begin to appreciate the significance of questions such as: Is this church organization characterized by trust or mistrust, alienation and polarization or reconciliation and respect for differences, rigidity or openness to new people and new ideas? Does this organization deal with differences honestly, or does it smother, bury, ignore, or treat them as though they were of no consequence? Does this organization deal with crises by retreating to past answers and solutions whether they are relevant or not, or does it accept the challenges posed and attempt to marshal the resources of its members to meet the challenges? Does it encourage *all* its members to contribute their ideas, energy, and commitments in ways that are satisfying to them and their Christian commitments, or does the leadership insist that there are only a selected number of program areas, tasks, and goals to which members must conform if they are to be useful to the organization?

Words such as "climate," "character," and "personality" of a church organization become important because they point to information available to people in those organizations. In the past we have concentrated upon duties, tasks, attainment of formal goals—raising a budget, obtaining a quota of new members, increasing attendance at worship services, meeting production schedules, etc. We have raised few questions about the consequences for people of the climate of a congregation or the character of a church organization. We have missed an obvious correlation between the climate of a congregation and participation in church activities. A minister can preach quite sophisticated and theologically "correct" sermons and never discover the discrepancy between his sermons and the climate of his congregation. Difficulty in raising the annual budget, poor attendance at congregational meetings, and apathy may have sources other than poor sermons.

Many church organizations are at war within them-

selves because their information is contradictory. The
words of the minister are contradicted by his organizational and community activities. The way committees and
church organizations are run is in direct contradiction to
the love, justice, and reconciliation written in the confessions and sung in hymns. Ministers and laymen have
become committed to their own private interests and
ends in the church, and the whole church suffers. The
question, Is the health, character, or climate of the church
organization a visible expression of Christian faith? is
seldom asked. Frequently, unhappy members drop out.
But mistrust, alienation, hostility, and a variety of thwarting behaviors may be overlooked as significant factors in
church life by both ministers and key leaders until the
intensity of such behavior increases so that it can no
longer be ignored.

If a minister is vaguely aware and somewhat uneasy
about this climate, he may conclude that his people are a
product of the times, or that *they* are the problem. Both
conclusions are partially true, but these conclusions miss
the point. As much time and energy need to be spent by
ministers, committees, and bureaucratic administrators
enabling the organization to be healthy, to have a climate
or character that more closely approximates its professed
Christian faith, as is spent preparing sermons, teaching,
and counseling.

What is at stake in the decision as to whether we shall
be churchmen, concerned about the nature of the information available to people in church organizations? We
do not have a complete answer to this question, but re-
search in two areas of organizational life, education and
business, suggests that everything that is important is at

stake: goals, means to goals, purposes, effective functioning as an organization.

The crisis in public education has confronted us with the reality that learning is a profound social, institutional phenomenon. Learning, as a behavior, is related to expectancies, norms, structures, and processes of classroom groups. The teacher and pupils together develop a climate that promotes and encourages learning or discourages and disrupts learning. The students as a group have a character that is different from the character of any single individual in the group. This corporate character defines and teaches students about teachers, subject matter, and learning activities. The definitions and teaching may be either negative or positive. Learning can be enhanced by these definitions or aggressive interruption and interference can take place. The teacher helps to create a climate for learning or unwittingly plays into the hands of the detractors through practices that define students and teachers, the activity, or the subject matter negatively.

Learning in the classroom is also related to the climate of the whole school organization. Styles of administrative leadership, administrative policies, programs of support for teachers or the lack of such programs, relations between administrators and faculty, administrators and students, faculty and students, are reflected in what takes place in the classroom. In a learning institution all personnel, policies, relationships, and programs have consequences for learning. No activity is neutral or without consequences in any educational system. Learning is influenced, supported, encouraged, by the total climate of an organization.

The fundamental purpose of education, teaching so that learning may occur, is at stake in the climate of an educational institution and the effects of this climate upon individuals and groups. This is true not only of public grade schools in both black and white communities but also of our institutions of higher education. (See especially Charles D. Orth, 3d, *et al., Social Structure and Learning Climate: The First Year at the Harvard Business School;* Harvard University Graduate School of Business Administration, 1963.)

Learning in a church through preaching-teaching, adult education courses, church school classes, and youth groups is likewise affected by the climate of the church organization and the climate of particular learning groups in the church. It is important to recognize that behavior, such as learning behavior, is not a response to a specific stimulus (as those experimental psychologists who have worked on rats and pigeons might suggest) but to an "image" of the environment as a whole (i.e., the climate). Human beings receive information from the whole organization and interpret this information in such a way as to develop ideas, attitudes, and values about the enterprises of that organization.

Since the early 1950's an impressive body of literature has developed that gives a great deal of information about the role and significance of climate upon persons, tasks, processes, and goals of contemporary organizations. Students of business and industry have discovered that the climate of an organization affects power, employee motivation at all levels, the need or lack of need for achievement, and social relationships. In other words, the climate has consequences for every aspect of organizational life. (See George H. Litwin and Robert A. Stringer, *Motivation and Organizational Climate;* Harvard University Graduate School of Business Administration, 1968.) Schools, business, and industry have learned that it is not sufficient to be concerned with particular behaviors, such as learning arithmetic or reading or producing a quota of items on an assembly line. The larger dimension of concern is with those conditions in an organization which encourage particular behaviors, such as trust, respect, reconciliation through resolution of conflict. These conditions are created. They are not natural to any organization, but rather are supported and encouraged by particular conditions within the institution.

Conditions that create expectancies, bring about positive learning, and encourage Christian thought and action are not widespread in church organizations. Most church organizations have been more concerned with task-oriented behavior and particular kinds of ethical, moral behavior than with the conditions that are necessary in an organization to encourage the development of such behaviors. In church organizations we urge, prophetically and frequently dogmatically, particular ethical behaviors in relation to race, peace, and poverty, rather than ask: What are the conditions, what is the nature of a church organization, that will support and encourage the development of particular kinds of ethical behavior?

We are prone to think that teaching by ministers and laity can be made effective merely by giving them a resource and a group of people. On occasion a group and teacher are brought together that are agreed on what is to be taught and what will be learned. Note what happens when the teacher and the group have disparate goals.

Continuing in the style of rugged individualism, the leader tells the others how to behave ethically, or what they ought to believe about the latest "in" theology while the "pupils" either fume inwardly, cause a disturbance, or let their minds wander. Frustration, skepticism, and polarization follow such attempts to teach when conditions for learning, for open disagreement, for openness to new ideas, and for a critical stance toward both old and new have not been created.

The experiences of students of public education, higher education, business, and industry suggest that far more attention must be given to the creation of conditions under which persons can change their behavior. This has meant a change in focus for leaders, managers, and educators. The focus is the whole organization and, in particular, the climate of that organization. Rugged individuals, whether in the church or the world, who concentrate exclusively upon "doing their own thing" (preaching, counseling, community activities) only compound the problems of their organization. They decrease the possibilities that the organization will be transformed to a more appropriate expression of Christian faith.

We need churchmen, managers, administrators, ministers, and laity who will be concerned about the conditions in their organizations that will support a whole range of behaviors—ethical activity inside and outside the church organization, effective ministry to those in need, effective teaching so that knowledge and faith commitments are shared, and better utilization of all interests, abilities, and commitments in the church.

There is little hope for either the church or the world if churchmen do not lead, manage, or administer church organizations so that the character of these organizations supports and affirms expressions of Christian faith and the work of people in worship, ministry, and mission.

It is no simple task to transform the climate of any organization. Knowledge, skill, and a great amount of energy are needed. Furthermore, the climate of any organization has a historical dimension. The past is always alive in the present structures and processes, and in the variety of values and faith commitments. The past is embedded in expectancies, styles of leadership, liturgical practices, and in preaching styles and content. Much of the past that we experience today was created by people who sought to give expression to Christian faith in their time. They were responsible people in their moment of history-making. Many of our difficulties today are due to our inability to be responsible history-making people in our time. We do not seem to be able to look at our history from the perspective of present faith commitments and see the inappropriateness for us of much of that created by men in previous generations. We have difficulty in understanding that Christian faith calls us to examine and transform the church organization in each new moment. There is a reticence to theologize—to think as Christians about the church itself.

Churchmen also encounter difficulty in transforming the church when those who give credit only to the present and reject all expressions from the past insist that only that which is totally new can meet the challenges of the present. No human organization and no churchmen seeking to transform that organization can escape the historical dimension and truly transform an organization when only the present informs the transforming process or the goals of transformation.

Faithfulness and the freedom of faith are manifest most when churchmen are truly historical men, realizing that Christian faith and the freedom found in this faith are not expressed when either the past or the present is made absolute. The Christian is most free and most faithful when he understands and acts upon his understanding of some anticipated future.

The church, consisting of a wide range of organizations, from local congregations, judicatories, and boards and agencies to ecumenical groups and councils, is called to transform its present and the past still alive in the present on the basis of a future, more adequate expression of Christian faith.

An understanding of Christian faith and life must serve to judge, guide, and direct our activity as churchmen in the transformation of our organizations. We must keep before us the object of transformation—the body of Christ. Our anticipated future, which is before us and yet serves in the present to give perspective to past and present, is the church organization as a visible, living expression of the body of Christ. The basis for transforming our current organizations is a theological one. Our theological commitments must find concrete expression in the corporate character or climate of our organization. The remaining chapters of this book will be an exploration of this task of churchmen.

4

A LIVING BODY
OR A DISMEMBERED CORPSE?

Long before anatomy and physiology were incorporated into the course work of every medical student, centuries before the circulatory system, the respiratory system, the nervous system, and other functioning body systems were discovered, and almost two thousand years before sixth- and seventh-grade children were studying the interdependency of all body parts and systems, Paul of Tarsus urged Christians to think of themselves as a corporate, organic body. This body, to be sure, had different parts. But each part was understood not in its own distinct shape or function, but in the manner in which each reflected, witnessed to, and pointed to the central purpose and function of the whole body. In each part both church and world could see the whole body's commitments, values, and purposes and the rule of the head, Jesus of Nazareth.

Paul was insistent that there can be no functional distinction between the body and that which motivates the body. No distinguishable souls or spirits separate from the body provide the essence of its life, nor do separate spirits or souls come to inhabit the body and then depart.

Rather, the various interrelated and interdependent parts, while specialized, diverse, and dissimilar in form and function, nevertheless reveal only the purposes, goals, and values of that which motivates the whole body, Jesus Christ.

Paul is not concerned that differences exist between parts. In fact, differences are viewed positively. The human body needs eyes, ears, arms, legs, and kidneys functioning together to do the work of the whole body. But the character or personality of the whole body is his dominant, overriding concern. From his Hebrew ancestors Paul learned that it is the social, corporate reality that is an expression of man's most fundamental commitments. It was the corporate organism that had such pronounced effect upon individuals, including Paul. Christians are not called to be individual Christians, but to be members of "a royal priesthood," "a holy nation," "the temple of the living God," members of the body of Christ. The most meaningful unit of Christian life for Paul, as for other New Testament writers, is the *corporate* body. This view represents a profound understanding of man, but it is easily understood by looking at our own life.

It is in corporate life that we are formed and transformed, sustained, encouraged, and given that which is necessary for life—both biologically and psychologically. The most meaningful unit of the life of a child is not life as an individual child, but life in corporate bodies such as the family, peer groups, and school. Later, in marriage, we are built up or destroyed, loved or hated, given hope or made to feel despair, in another corporate relationship. We find either fulfillment or despair both in life and in work because of the corporate character or personality of our work situation. The significance of the corporate nature of our life ought to be such a stark reality for us that we no longer engage in that meaningless exercise of arguing whether we are solitary individuals or social creatures. We are both individual and social, distinct parts and members of a body. We cannot separate these two aspects of our life.

Paul's only concern was that Christians live as the body of Christ, that the church, the body of Christ, recognize in itself Christ in his work. Robinson states this point as clearly as possible in his study of Paul's understanding of the body of Christ:

> It is almost impossible to exaggerate the materialism and crudity of Paul's doctrine of the church as literally now the resurrection *body* of Christ. The language of "membership" of a body corporate has become so trite that the idea that the individual can be a "member" has ceased to be offensive. The force of Paul's words can today perhaps be got only by paraphrasing: "Ye are the body of Christ and severally membranes thereof" (I Cor. 12.27). The body that he has in mind is as concrete and as singular as the body of the Incarnation. His underlying conception is not of a supra-personal collective, but of a specific personal organism. He is not saying anything so weak as that the church is a society with a common life and governor, but that its unity is that of a single physical entity: disunion is dismemberment. (J.A.T. Robinson, *The Body*, p. 51; London: SCM Press, Ltd., 1957.)

The body of Christ, the church, is the physical expression of the work of the head, Jesus Christ! It was this body which Paul experienced and which led to his own conversion. In the church that he persecuted, Paul saw Christ. This living Christ, the Church, called him to be one with it, a part of the body. It is easy to appreciate Paul's primary concern for the creation of the body of Christ on his missionary journeys and among the young churches when we understand that it was the Christ living in his people that turned his own life around so dramatically. The carrier of new life to Paul was a people who had a Lord and knew themselves to be the physical, living resurrection of that Lord.

As we live amid the dismembered corporate bodies of our world, Paul's understanding of the body of Christ may seem to be sheer romanticism. It may be! But we have no optional understandings that give us hope as men and women who are the products of a world of polarization and disunion. In this world, church people as the body of Christ must be far more conscious of their life and thought as a compelling alternative for man. Self-awareness and deliberateness in creating and maintaining its own life ought to characterize the church today. This involves honestly confronting our most crucial problems and dealing with them, for otherwise there can be no reconciliation among members of the body and, hence, no true body of Christ.

Our division, dismemberment, and polarization are seen most frequently in our answers to the questions: What is appropriate individual Christian behavior? and What is the church? Let's consider them separately. First, what *is* appropriate Christian behavior?

From the immediate past we can note a variety of customs—no smoking, no drinking, particular dress customs, patterns of prayer, Bible-reading, and church attendance. We have absolutized, for all times and places, many of these past customs only because they are the customs most visible to us. We do not see the range of behaviors of Christians during past centuries.

The Gospels and the writings of Paul are full of illustrations of diversity and the lively discussions and debates over appropriate individual Christian behavior within the first-century church. Strangely enough, early Christians had problems with dress, food, drinking, sexual behavior, relation to the larger culture, attendance and behavior in worship, relations between faith and ethics. The most fundamental issue facing early Christians was whether the new pious Christian behavior was an overlay of Jewish pious behavior, or whether a new Christian behavior was to emerge as a result of the new freedom in Christ.

The early church people never settled their problems. The differences in the Gospels and the writings of Paul are an everlasting witness to the fact that they learned to live and appreciate the pluralism of early Christianity. The evidence for this is the inclusion of all their differences as their mutual, corporate record. They understood that *with* their differences they were the church, the body of Christ.

The most striking feature of this pluralism of ideas as to what constituted Christian behavior is that all the ideas were qualified, informed, and judged by an understanding of the work, person, or teachings of Jesus of Nazareth. No matter whether individual Christian behavior looked like a modified form of Greek or Jewish life, the significant feature was that early Christians were actually trying to *think and act* as Christians. The writers and editors of the New Testament noticed this and preserved it. Study of the New Testament today reveals the multiplicity and diversity of early Christian theologies and the behaviors resulting from them.

If Christians today perceive that we are in some historical, continuous relationship with the nature and character of the early church, then our theologies and our behaviors will be likewise multiple and diverse. The criterion is the same for us as for the early church. We too must think and behave as Christians, as the body of Christ. However, rather than recognize honest searching for the meaning of Christian faith today with its consequences for individual behavior, too often we declare one another the enemy. We take sides and attempt to make the other side an absolute loser and ourselves absolute winners. Conservatives, liberals, and others who don't know what they are refuse to acknowledge that the body of Christ must have diversity of ideas, functions, and commitments.

Perhaps to appreciate this fact we must more fully understand the Pauline concept of the body of Christ. "For just as the body is one and has many members, and all the members of the body, though many, are one body, so it is with Christ." (I Cor. 12:12.) Christ is a unity, as is the human body. Christ as the church or the church as Christ is one body, no matter how many members it has or how diverse these members may be in their functions or ideas. There can be no body with only one member. There must be many members. There must be different members if there is to be a body (I Cor. 12:14). The body of Christ can and must function in diversity. Yet while it functions in diversity, there is only one body of Christ. The various members with different ideas and functions need only to discern that they have a common source for their ideas and actions, Jesus of Nazareth, and are, therefore, bound together as members of his body. "Because there is one bread, we who are many are one body, for we all partake of the one bread." (I Cor. 10:17.)

We scarcely appreciate the diversity and conflict among the fledgling churches that Paul was attempting to establish. Throughout his writings he attempts to share with these churches a theological understanding of who they are as people, that they might be enabled to live with their differences. He states in numerous ways: "For as in one body we have many members, and all the members do not have the same function, so we, though many, are one body in Christ, and individually members one of another" (Rom. 12:4-5).

We are confronted with the same reality as the early church. We are one body with one Lord. Our problem is to recognize this fact and then discuss and decide together how we shall live as one body with our differences. The fifteenth chapter of The Acts is a remarkable record of a gathering of the diverse early church in council at Jerusalem to discuss and decide together how they would live together in diversity and dependency. The council agreed to bless Paul's understanding of the ministry. They supported him even though they could not engage in radically new and different ministry themselves. The activities and ideas of the council of Jerusalem ought to characterize every local church, judicatory, board, and agency as we decide how to live with our different understandings of appropriate Christian behavior and our different ideas about the church and its mission. The honesty and openness with which the issues were set forth, the candor of discussion, and the ability to arrive at a decision in which no person acting out of honest Christian convictions was made an absolute loser are characteristics of that council held so long ago which seem desperately needed today. These attributes of that early body of Christ ought to judge and inform our church life today.

The second and equally divisive question in our lives is, What does it mean to be the church? We, as a church, are as divided as the church has ever been by our competing and conflicting ideas of who we are.

One group among us maintains that the primary concern of ministers and church members is with the individual lives of Christians. The church cares for its own and lives in hope that the world will be saved by people joining the church and becoming members of the saved community. The task of preaching, teaching, worship services, and church life is to enable church members to live in the world individually as Christians, and to have their primary effect upon the world as individuals. The stance of the church toward the world is primarily therapeutic. Wars, riots, poverty, juvenile delinquency, drug use, and other social conditions are met through programs that pick up the pieces after social catastrophe has occurred. Food, clothing, gang workers, social workers, and settlement houses are provided to treat the victims. Professional ministry and the activity of laymen in the church are directed primarily toward personal crises of members (i.e., marriage counseling, ministry to the elderly, coffeehouse ministries, and youth ministries).

This individual-oriented group mirrors the culturally

designated role of the church. The church is for personal crises and for therapeutic treatment of social catastrophe. Those in this first group (among them many politicians, educators, businessmen, and labor leaders) declare that the church is meddling, is not taking care of the "spiritual life," when Christians begin to probe to the roots of problems in our society rather than dealing strictly with individuals.

A second and equally committed group insists that the primary concern of the church is how God rules in the world. They feel that Christians should be more interested in preventing disease than in treating it. They search for root causes rather than symptoms in order that they may show God's care for the world. They are more interested in preventing social crises than treating personal crises; hence they object to much of the traditional ministry. They have much less concern for maintaining the church as an institutionally effective witness than for witnessing themselves in the world.

This latter group points to the personal crisis, pastoral, clergy orientation of the church as a witness to the agrarian past. Their concern is with an urban, technological society in which men are creating a world where men organize men and machines to change our world and us. Men are creators of social relations and institutions. Nowhere, they claim, does the solitary individual exist who can influence the world of technology and institutions as a solitary good man. These churchmen have difficulty understanding the relevance or appropriateness of the past, individualistic understanding of church and mission, and they insist that much of life is lived in contradiction to that understanding.

They point, for example, to the first summary section of the *Report of the National Advisory Commission on Civil Disorders:* "What white Americans have never fully understood—but what the Negro can never forget—is that white society is deeply implicated in the ghetto. White institutions created it, white institutions maintain it, and white society condones it." White Christians, they charge, are in the strange position of having created men and a world for men through their corporate, institutional life, then piously declaring to themselves that there is no Christian basis for judging or changing that creation.

Because the church seems so unaware of the effects of its actions as corporate, institutional men, many in this second group doubt that we have the capacity or will to judge our creations and change them. This is what many thoughtful high school and college students mean when they charge that the system is sick and the whole system must go. They mean that white Christianity has created a world based upon ideas about the church and Christian behavior that are no longer pertinent or relevant to the world. In fact, they claim that we and our ideas are the enemy. Most of the young people who make this claim are our own children.

The realities of our world only increase these tensions between liberals and conservatives, young and old, clergy and laity, precisely at the moment when we need all the resources of the faith commitments of people—young, old, rich, poor, liberal, conservative, black, white, clergy, and laity—to be the diversified unified body of Christ in the world. No single group has the energy, ideas, programs, economic resources, or faith commitments to be effective sole agent of reconciliation in our world.

We, churchmen, are creating a world. There is no doubt about that. Our problem is far greater than merely judging or following our past understanding of Christian behavior, church life, and mission. We must get beyond our past creations and face the dimensions of the creating we have to do in the present and future world—a world in which it is impossible to retreat to the behaviors and ideas of the past or simply to react to present problems.

We are faced with the force and significance of our life as history-making people. We are making ourselves and others today, creating the conditions for a continual shaping of ourselves and others in the future. We are confronted with social crises that demand solutions other than the paternal, personal, therapeutic activities of the past. At this moment we must be concerned about our involvement in changing the world and others. Perhaps more important, we must find a new self-understanding, as individuals and churchmen, that leads to changing ourselves.

The divisiveness and polarization existing in the church cannot be tolerated by Christians. If it is, we are dead. We are a dismembered corpse. To allow our different understandings of the nature of the church to paralyze us, to dismember us, to make us no body of Christ, is intolerable in the light of our history.

A living body of Christ has *always* had two foci, itself and the world. We ought to have discovered this from our study of the Pauline writings. Paul's concern is twofold. First, for that body which is dynamic and which has parts functioning together. This body pays attention to itself, appreciates and builds upon the contribution of all members. It cares, really cares, for all its members, feeding, supporting, and sustaining those diverse parts. It is self-directed and raises critical questions about its parts and how they function. It is involved in personal crises. Any personal crisis is a threat to the whole body and the functioning of the body as the body of Christ.

But Paul is also concerned for the *missionary* body of Christ, which is noted for what it is and does. The missionary body of Christ is of fundamental consequence for the *world*. The living parts, working together, are the source of nurture, change, judgment, and direction of the world. The body is sent into the world: "Come to him . . . and like living stones be yourselves built into a spiritual house, to be a holy priesthood" (I Peter 2:4, 5).

The early church was described as "a chosen race," "a royal priesthood," "a holy nation," "God's own people." Its task was to live as God's people in the world. We do not appreciate the imagery or the meaning carried in these words for early Christians. Interpreted today they mean that we are an organic, living group who are to examine our group life in the light of our common calling to be the living embodiment of God's work in the world. We are to have a character, a personality *as a people*, not just as individuals, because we are a chosen race as well as chosen individuals. We are a royal priesthood as we are a group of people healing, sacrificing, reconciling, redeeming, and judging the world. We are a holy nation, we Christians, as we live as a corporate people in relation to the world. The choice is not really between individual life and corporate life, or individual Christian behavior and church behavior, or church and world.

5
TOWARD A THEOLOGY
OF THE INSTITUTIONAL CHURCH

To start, the church is confused. Those who are determined to preserve the institution are battling those who are equally determined to find self-expression and individual fulfillment and who see the institutional church as stifling their creativity. Each side clings to what it "knows"—instinctively—is right but neither can explain exactly why the other side is wrong—why an institution is more important than the people who make it up or how people can express themselves corporately without creating an institution.

Churchmen desperately need a theological mandate as they create and guide the functioning organizations that must care for, nourish, and sustain men as they live as members of these organizations and as they extend their lives into the world. There is much talk about the creation of "missionary structures" among clergy, accompanied by disdain and contempt for the institutional church. But these discussions are remarkably naïve. The institutional church is dead, they say, and therefore, out of nothing, new missionary structures must emerge that are appropriate expressions of Christian faith today.

Spontaneous generation was refuted with the work of Pasteur. All new life comes from preexisting life. But this means that the institutional church must be taken far more seriously than it has been in the past. Clergy and laity must be prepared to think theologically, functionally, and practically about church organizations. Few know how to help an organization transform and renew itself. Our concern must be for the conditions in organizations that allow particular forms of new life to emerge, and we must be doubly concerned about a theological mandate, a stance informed by Christian faith, that enhances and promotes true care for the church and the world.

We can no longer be content with the current prophetic trend that says the church is dead or dying. This will paralyze us and allow us to escape from confronting who we are as clergy and laity in relation to the church and the world. There is no room, theologically or practically, for the idea that if the institutional church would just die, a new, free, appropriate form of Christianity would emerge—that is, a noninstitutional Christian form. Radical Protestants, conservative and liberal, exhibit a decided preference for free-floating, nonconnectional, sectarian, like-minded, warm ingroups as the "real" expression of Christian faith. Yet the commitment to this form of church life and world occurs at a moment when we have just begun to appreciate the institutional nature of every aspect of life. We have begun also to appreciate the interdependent nature of all institutional life, and particularly of those institutions which provide centers of values and commitments in a rapidly changing society.

In any society, movements for change must become part of organizations. As such, they must become part of the contribution of that organization to the organizations it touches through its members and through its common life as an organization. Utopian, sectarian, and protest groups eventually enter the mainstream of life, or they die. They are incorporated by organizations, effect the transformations of those organizations, and maximize their commitments and concerns through organizational life. There are few, if any, noninstitutional forms of life that are capable of being effective in their relations over an extended period of time. The establishment of patterns of structures, relationships, communication and decision-making processes, and some value or ideological basis seems necessary for sustained life and maximum effect on other organizations. Institutionalization seems necessary for significant, long-range involvement in transforming society.

The most contemporary example of this phenomenon is the civil rights movement, which now has entered the phase of seeking to institutionalize, to make its goals and values regular parts of organizations as rapidly as possible. Its emphasis on political, educational, economic, and religious institutions shows the sophistication and development of a people who are aware that being right is not the same as being effective. Effectiveness means the transformation of organizations. The rise of black theology responds to the need for a value center, a source to inform and direct the transformation of organizations. The black militant churchman is an excellent example of a concerned person who knows that institutions cannot be demolished but, rather, must be transformed into just, caring institutions.

In the same way, Protestant churchmen must now turn

to the institutional church to transform it into that value center appropriate to a tumultuous society. It is theologically and practically unsound for us to live as Christians whose focus is primarily upon our own lives and the lives of our families. Yet this is the way most of us live. We actually care little for the body of Christ as it is visible in the institutional church. We have almost no concern for how this body cares for itself and others. Ministers, laymen, and church administrators have their own agendas that take precedence over their care for the institutional church as the body of Christ and the missionary body of Christ in the world.

Something has been missing from our self-understanding as churchmen—an understanding of the church as an institution that through its very life gives expression to its commitments, values, and interests. We have something to learn from contemporary Roman Catholic scholars who understand that the church as an institution ought to be an incarnate expression of Christian faith. The discussions within Roman Catholicism that set forth new structures and processes for decision-making and communication, new relations between clergy and laity, hierarchy ought to serve as a stimulus for rethinking our own understanding of the institutional church. The discussions of these scholars are informed by that Biblical scholarship which searches for the meaning of the church, and a fresh understanding of the role and function of the people of God, and the body of Christ, in the Old and New Testament records. Biblical and theological reflection about institutional church life is providing a major impetus to the reformation of Roman Catholic life and thought today.

Hans Küng, manifesting a profound concern for the very nature of ecumenical councils, attempts to show how Christian theology, which is informed by the revelation of God in Jesus Christ, has something concrete to say to ecumenical councils through enabling churchmen to "penetrate to the very nature of ecumenical councils" (*Structures of the Church*, tr. by Salvator Attansio; Thomas Nelson & Sons, 1964). Küng and his fellow Catholic scholars want *every* aspect of church life, including councils, to become a visible expression of Christian faith.

There are more similarities between Protestants and Roman Catholics than either group cares to admit. Both share the tendency to let the institutional church with its hierarchy, status positions, committee structures, and political processes determine the work of the Spirit of God. Both Protestants and Catholics have had difficulty in letting unexpected, new, and creative expressions of Christianity become visible sources of new life in the institutional church. Ministers, laymen, and church administrators have attempted to set limits on the work of the Spirit of God by appealing to tradition, the latest theology, or the needs of the world. Yet, as Karl Rahner has stated unambiguously: "It is not possible to conceive the official church and hierarchy as the institutional organizer and administrator of the gift of the Spirit in the church, unless one sees her from the start as being herself, she the lawgiving church, first and foremost the Church of the Charismata" (Holy Spirit). (*The Dynamic Element in the Church*, p. 61; Herder & Herder, Inc., 1964.)

The church is first the church of the Spirit—innovative, freely giving and receiving, open to the present and the future. As such it must seek always to give expression to truth, the work of its head, Jesus Christ, and the work of the Spirit in its institutional life. Relations between clergy and laity, clergy and clergy, laity and laity, and church and world should follow from Christian faith rather than exist as static entities to which faith, Spirit, and grace conform. Church organizations must always exist dynamically, being transformed as faith, Spirit, and grace find appropriate expression.

Another similarity between Protestants and Roman Catholics is pointed out by Michael Novak, one of the most vigorous spokesmen in the United States for a transformation of church structures. He sees present church structures as inhibiting people from becoming themselves. Structures are needed that promote an environment for supporting persons in their differences. This means that just structures must be created whereby all can share their gifts, structures that will allow for common concerns to be mobilized and acted upon, and that will maintain the conditions under which conflicts can be resolved and reconciliation can occur in institutional church structures.

Structures appropriate to the new conditions of our world must

> allow an *environment,* in which such aberrations can exist, for the sake of a deeper kind of freedom. It is to allow the individual person "to sink or swim" and to encourage individuals to become persons, to show individuals *how* "to swim." It is, above all, to emphasize that each individual must become a person by himself; no one can force him to do so; no one else can do it for him. There is no way of mass-producing persons. There is no "new structure" that will automatically reform and renew persons. Indi-

viduals [merely] can be "formed" by structures: persons develop chiefly from within, often against the pressures of social structures.

To become a person is to become faithful to one's own insights, and to be faithful to all the claims to one's own unrestricted drive to understand. ("Diversity of Structures and Freedom Within Structures," *Dogma*, p. 107, Vol. I of *Concilium: Theology in the Age of Renewal*, ed. by Edward Schillebeeckx; Paulist Press, 1964.)

Novak argues that the traditional structures of the Catholic Church are based upon an erroneous understanding of man. They do not show "sufficient confidence in the human person" as a complex, contemporary creature who can no longer be satisfied with the limited understanding of Christian faith manifested in the concrete life of the church. Present structures do not allow persons to contribute what they uniquely can contribute, their faith commitments, energy, imagination, and concern for both the church and the world. The church itself, he might say, is dehumanizing. It does not allow men to share with one another what is most characteristic of being human, the insight, imagination, creativity, thoughtfulness, and faith of men.

Criticism of and concern for the structures of the church and their consequences for persons are valid not only for Roman Catholics but for Protestants as well. The gifts of persons are wasted in every church organization. In fact, no church organization really knows what it possesses in the faith commitments, interests and concern, innovative possibilities, and economic resources of all its members. Church organizations waste the human gifts available to them on a fantastic scale. As pragmatic people we think we know most about the economic resources of people. It is not until we begin to understand the relations between motivation, concerns, and faith commitments that we become aware of the vast untapped economic resources in the churches. We are grossly unaware of the other gifts, latent and potential, in church organizations.

In the call for new structures by many in church organizations there is a distinct secondary echo calling for the revitalization of leaders and the transformation of relationships between persons in any new structures. Roman Catholic churchmen have been more specific and, perhaps, more courageous in calling for greater responsiveness by and different relationships with those in status, hierarchical, and power positions as a visible expression of Christian faith. The issues of birth control, decision-making in diocesan areas, the authority of bishops and priests, reveal the tensions and the transformations at work in the Roman Catholic Church.

This same desire for a more concerned and just leadership that can enter into new reconciling and reciprocal relations with all members of church organizations is expressed by Protestants. It can be seen in increasingly tense relations among bishops, clergy, and people, among judicatories, boards, agencies, and local church ministers and laymen. It is especially seen in the growing anticlericalism of Protestantism. Underneath much of the tension and frustration is a desire of laymen and ministers for a more human organization, a church organization that defines them as persons and that seeks to elicit their gifts for sharing with others.

The cultural era is over, finished, when bishops, church executives, district superintendents, or judicatory officials can decide which gifts of which people the church will use. The features of our culture described in Chapter 2 are doing their work so that the old conditions that supported static, hierarchical organizations, unilateral decision-making, and unidirectional communication can never develop again. A new, fraternal, collaborative relationship must emerge that enables persons with their variety of gifts to decide mutually how, when, and which gifts will be used, or the church organization will die.

Dying is already taking place. When people believe that an organization with its ideas, values, and knowledge is important for them, they refuse to let that organization die. They become actively aggressive in attempting to change it so that its ideas, values, knowledge, and meaning will be appropriate. But when children, young people, and adults conclude that an organization is inappropriate and irrelevant, they become passively aggressive. They drop out. They reduce their commitments and energy. Motivation diminishes. Silence becomes the symptom pointing to this tendency toward death.

Most church people live in an ambiguous state between active and passive aggression. If the commitment tips to passive aggression, as the increasing signs of silence suggest—difficulty in obtaining church officers, low attendance at annual meetings, withholding of pledges by both liberals and conservatives, difficulty in staffing church educational enterprises, distrust and suspicion between different units of the church—then dying is already upon an organization. Death is only a matter of time unless the leadership is renewed and revitalized and a transformation takes place in the relations of leaders with others in the organization.

One visible expression of the church as the body of Christ, which has need for the gifts of all its members, is our current Protestant reliance upon Roman Catholic scholars for help in responding to our own institutional crisis. The strength and appropriateness of their aid is based upon their understanding of the organizational church as a place for the manifestation of God's work in Christ in the world. Edward Schillebeeckx states unequivocally: "The visible Church itself is the Lord's mystical body." (*Christ, the Sacrament of the Encounter with God,* p. 48; Sheed & Ward, Inc., 1963.)

Catholic scholars have pointed to real, experienced facets of institutional church life—structures, relationships, and the content of faith—and have suggested that these need to be informed and transformed by Christian faith. Using the concepts developed in an earlier chapter, we can say that the character, personality, climate, of the church is where grace, faith, and truth are visible. The greater the congruency between the life of the institutional church and its ministry and mission as the work of Christ, the more we can say, as Edward Schillebeeckx has suggested, that the Word is the church itself ("Revelation in Word and Deed," *The Word: Readings in Theology,* ed. by Carney Gavin, *et al.,* p. 262; P. J. Kenedy & Sons, 1964).

At first glance it may seem that contemporary Catholic scholars are still "putting the church in the place of God," as Protestants have long contended. There is a much more important insight to gain from these scholars that ought to enable us to reject that ancient prejudice. These scholars are primarily concerned with *God's* rule over the church, the institutional church as a living, visible expression of his work in Christ in the world. The task they have before them as Christian theologians is to think about the people of God as these people are gathered in human institutions called churches. Their purpose is to discover the forms, relationships, and contents of faith appropriate for his people today if they are to live as faithful witnesses doing *Christ's work in the church and the world.* The emphasis and dominant concern is upon God's work in Christ. And the only form at hand for the continuance of this work is the institutional church.

The basis for transformation of the church is not fad or program, but a theological understanding of how God is at work among his people, and how his people can respond in this day and time as they continue his work. To proceed in this manner is to open the church to deep and fundamental examination of all that is and has been. Theological reflection and criticism moves the church beyond custom, tradition, or fad as answers to church ministry and mission. Answers come not from the church but from that which transcends the church and judges, directs, and informs its life—the Word of God become flesh, Jesus Christ. Answers to questions, solutions to problems, come to Christians as, openly in trust and hope, they together attempt to discern the meaning of the Word become flesh in their flesh, and in their gathered flesh as church.

This positive affirmation of Catholic theological thought is not meant to imply that there are no significant problems or differences with their ideas. For one thing, there is a theological pressure to make the present

hierarchical structure defensible in relation to the early-
church concept of the body of Christ. This shows clearly
the difficulty of theological reflection that has to deal
with custom and tradition as well as with New Testament
life and present realities.

The significance of the body in Pauline thought is not
structure, but functioning as the body with a head, Jesus
Christ. Proper functioning takes place only when there is
true interdependency of parts, where all parts are working together as parts of the whole. The weaker and less
presentable parts are given greater honor, so that God
gives "greater honor to the inferior part, that there may
be no discord in the body, but that the members may
have the same care for one another. If one member suffers, all suffer together; if one member is honored, all re-
joice together" (I Cor. 12:24-26). The concept of the
body of Christ will not support the idea of structurally
arranged hierarchy in the institutional church in which
power, authority, ideas, and status flow from the top
down. This concept suggests, rather, that power, authority, ideas, energy, and motivation flow from different
parts, depending upon which gifts the body has need of
at the moment.

A second major difference is a cultural one. Theories of
leadership and organization arise from a cultural milieu,
and ideas and styles of organization and leadership have
a dynamic and reciprocal relation to a given culture. Cultural ideas and styles influence church organizations and
vice versa. Feudalism was manifested in both church and
society by a rigid hierarchy, static relationship, power,
status, and authority lodged at the top with little recourse
from the decisions made there. Roman Catholics and

Protestants (only to a lesser degree) formalized and routinized this concept of organization and leadership.

Today both Catholics and Protestants are experiencing challenges to this past understanding of organization and the theology that legitimatized this understanding. A new cultural era has arrived with new ideas about organizations and leadership. Yet Catholic scholars are attempting to combine the theories of organization from the past with a contemporary Biblical and theological understanding of the church.

In this book another course is pursued. We are working toward a contemporary Biblical and theological understanding of the institutional church and ministry that takes into account a contemporary understanding of human organizations. The aim is to bring a theological understanding of the church and a theory of organization and leadership together so that the contemporary church may become a visible expression of the faith commitments of Christians in its ministry and mission.

A serious study of the New Testament ought to settle the debate about our split character. Scripture speaks strong words to the easy solution of problems by polarizing and separating individuals and groups from one another. Polarization and alienation are "copping out," as young people describe retreat today. There is no honest confrontation, no reconciliation, no maximization and optimization of one another's resources, no judgment of one another, when we take the easy road—retreat to our enclave of like-minded people.

The body of Christ with Jesus of Nazareth as its head is both individual and world-oriented. The question for churchmen is not whether we are engaged in the world, but how we will be in the world as the body of Christ. Our energy, our debates, our commitments, ought to focus upon answering this question. This is the legitimate question for Christians to answer. The answers to this question have the greatest consequence for the world.

To be true to the Pauline understanding of the body of Christ, we must recognize that there is never a time when we act as individuals out of our own goodness and wisdom. We are always members of the body and acting as the body in the world. We continue the purposes, the work, of God in Jesus Christ, in the world. It is the missionary body of Christ that works in the world, not missionaries sent to do our work. We are the missionary body of Christ in the world. There are no other real missionaries. It is the institutional church living as a people with a head, Jesus Christ, that is the missionary in the world. No clergyman can be hired to be our missionary. We are missionaries as we are suffering, sacrificing, judging, redeeming, and reconciling God's world to him. No one can do that for us!

We cannot be one-sided, theoretical, or dogmatic in our understanding of the body of Christ. The church is too full of people who have not sought for a depth of understanding of the meaning of the corporate life of the body. Both liberals and conservatives have been more concerned with the rhetoric that maintains their own historic position than with subjecting that position to Scriptural and theological criticism. The consequence of this separatist activity is a dismembered body, a body that can take care of neither itself nor the world.

In this interdependent, astonishingly rapid-changing world, the body needs diverse members that function as parts of the whole body. One source of hope in the world is a body of Christ that cares for both itself and the world. We will have to transform our present existence as a "holy nation" if we are to care for ourselves and the world. The basis for this transformation is an understanding of ourselves as the body of Christ, which has two foci, ourselves and others. This self-understanding needs to find expression in the contemporary institutional church if this church is to be an expression of Christian faith. We turn now to look at the institutional church.

6

TOWARD AN UNDERSTANDING
OF ORGANIZATIONS—I

Since 1955, theory about organizations has developed at an accelerating pace. The development of post-World War II technology, the increasing pluralism of environments of organizations, and the development of new theoretical concepts such as those provided by systems theory have resulted in new theory and practice in organizations.

One of the early profound insights to emerge was that of the organization as an "interpretive system." (Tom Burns and G. M. Stalker, *The Management of Innovation;* London: Tavistock Publications, Ltd., 1961.) Organizations are living systems, interrelated and interdependent, which interpret and define mission, task, purposes, priorities, people, relationships, authority structures, relation to environment, use of resources, commitments, and motivation. Meanings are given by one part of the organization to every other part of the organization. Interpretation of every aspect of organizational life is taking place throughout the whole organization. No part is autonomous, independent, isolated, and without effect for other parts. The whole organization is a vast store of information interpreting every aspect of organizational life (see Chapter 3).

The second major breakthrough in understanding organizations came with the development of a universal open-system model. This model is universal in that it can be used to gain understanding of any human organization from the family to the largest corporation. The openness of the organization points to the interdependent relation of any organization with its environment. Different environments provide different people, resources, traditions, and conditions. The environment is a crucial input into every organization. No organization is self-sufficient. (See Albert K. Rice, *The Enterprise and Its Environment;* London: Tavistock Publications, Ltd., 1963.)

Church organizations can be understood by using such a model.

Every church organization is an input system. It incorporates, filters, and directs people, money, ideas, etc. In local churches incorporation is seen in new membership classes, stewardship and evangelism programs, and family nights. Filters operate to incorporate some people into particular programs, groups, or decision-making processes, and to exclude others from these same opportunities for a variety of reasons. Money is filtered, so that disproportionate amounts are spent on buildings, paid choirs, organs, educational programs, and ministry and mission programs. Personal values, self-interests, organizational interests, and theological commitments influence the nature and character, efficiency and effectiveness, of the input, incorporating system.

In addition, the historical and existential dimensions of a church's environment have substantial consequences in

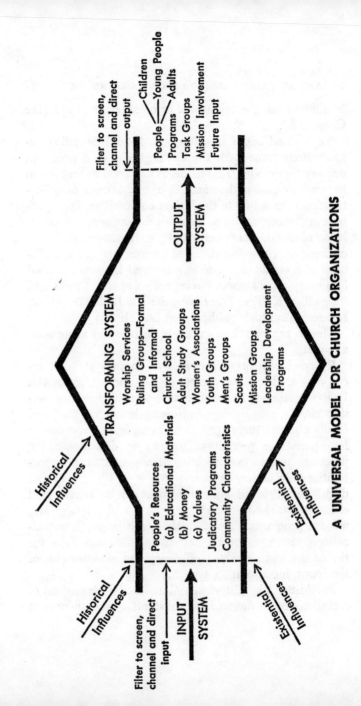

A UNIVERSAL MODEL FOR CHURCH ORGANIZATIONS

INPUT SYSTEM

Filter to screen, channel and direct input

Historical Influences

Existential Influences

People's Resources
(a) Educational Materials
(b) Money
(c) Values
Judicatory Programs
Community Characteristics

TRANSFORMING SYSTEM

Historical Influences

Existential Influences

Worship Services
Ruling Groups—Formal and Informal
Church School
Adult Study Groups
Women's Associations
Youth Groups
Men's Groups
Scouts
Mission Groups
Leadership Development Programs

OUTPUT SYSTEM

Filter to screen, channel and direct output

People
  Children
  Young People
  Adults
Programs
Task Groups
Mission Involvement
Future Input

terms of input. Every church organization has some degree of commitment to tradition, custom, and historical experience. The organization also is affected by the conditions in which it exists—community crises, gangs, drug use by adolescents, urban renewal, loss of people (particularly college-age adults and young families in small towns), or industries moving into a community (bringing people with new ideas and fewer commitments to community traditions). Frequently, the historical and existential dimensions of church life are sources of tension, frustration, and polarization in church life. Controlling powers in the churches may attempt to meet crises from a turbulent environment by tightening control of both the input and the groups within the church.

Church organizations also have transforming systems—groups that have tasks and functions in relation to particular people and resources. The transforming system of churches is primarily an educational, caring system (note the diagram on page 78). Each group (or subsystem) has a primary task of caring for either people in the group, the whole church organization, or some aspect of the world.

Modern systems theory maintains that every subsystem has consequences for every other subsystem and the whole organization. If the worship service, including preaching, is not meaningful, the whole church suffers and every group suffers. If ruling groups are dominated by self-interest, every group is deprived of energy, resources, ideas, and people. If the adult study program is inadequate, the church school and young people's groups do not have a source of well-equipped adults who understand Christian faith and who can interpret and express this faith to children and adults. If there are no significant leadership development programs, every group suffers from the paucity of leadership skills and knowledge. If ministry and mission groups are weak or nonexistent, the whole organization becomes ingrown, individualistic, and self-centered. Young people are deprived of the relevant definitions and meanings of Christian faith vis à vis the world. They are given an extremely narrow and one-sided understanding of the church and in fact may be taught heresy by the life of the church—that the body of Christ is of little or no consequence for church members or the world.

Various subsystems or groups doing their tasks well as members of the body of Christ mean life and hope to one another and to the whole body. But if the women's association, adult study groups, ministry and mission groups, or any of the various ruling groups conclude they are self-sufficient, independent, not responsible for others, then every other group—and the whole organization—becomes sick. Organizational theorists write of sick and healthy organizations. Some of the signs of health are group interdependency, maximum use of human and other resources in various groups to achieve their goals, each group's ability to perform its tasks for the welfare of the whole organization, ability to resolve conflict between persons and groups, and ability to pursue the mission and purposes of an organization.

Using these criteria for evaluation of church organization, we would discover that most church organizations are sick. The number of people who are alienated or lonely and who become cynical and bitter in church organizations would shock most power structures if they did a diagnosis of their organizations. Church organizations are rarely characterized by reconciliation in which differences are lifted up, made highly visible, and worked on until conflict is resolved and people learn to live together mutually sharing their gifts. Yet the alienated and lonely have unmeasured resources of energy, commitment, ideas, and values that go unwanted and unused in the body of Christ.

Output systems in church organizations are the most unorganized, chaotic, and troublesome. They are troublesome primarily because of our Protestant commitment to individualism. We produce individuals and individual churches that sink or swim on their own without support, nurture, or care from a larger body while they are responding to needs of the world.

We do the most to support persons as they leave local churches to attend colleges and universities. Through the ministry of chaplains and university pastors, we follow young people from local churches and communities to higher education institutions with the ministry and mission of the church. The greatest innovativeness in support of mission and ministry can be seen on those campuses where care and support reaches out not only through direct ministry to students, but to faculty, administrators, and the organization of higher education.

Experimental ministries to businesses and industries are also forms of support for persons in the decision-making processes of these sectors of life. We have only begun to explore the alternatives for nurturing, caring, and supporting persons in ministry and mission. The most important requirement of every organization is that such support, nurture, and care be fraternal and cooperative rather than paternal, unilateral, and controlled.

In the past, local churches, judicatories and particularly boards and agencies have expressed a desire to nurture both individuals and lower rungs in the hierarchy. But nurture was equated with control, and since they had no means to control, individuals and congregations were left to their own devices. Frequently boards and judicatory officials have even concluded that local churches and individuals were the enemy when they requested support, care, and nurture through programs and resources that deviated from those prescribed. One of the major challenges to be met by church organizations in the '70s will be the development of support and caring programs to maintain persons in the total, diversified ministry and mission of the church.

7

TOWARD AN UNDERSTANDING
OF ORGANIZATIONS—II

Every subsystem, group, or organization has three aspects: structure, processes, and content. These three are the building blocks of every organization. Let's consider them separately.

STRUCTURE: THE CONTEXT OF ORGANIZATIONAL LIFE

Most church people seeking to change the church have viewed the formal structure as the crucial variable to be changed. Greatest attention has been given to structure in church literature. The panacea for all ills has become "Change the structure."

There is no doubt that the structure of any organization is important, but it is only one part of that which makes up the organization. The given, "formal" structure of an organization consists of the manner in which formal authority and power are distributed among members of an organization. Structure designates areas of responsibility and accountability for the performance of tasks such as establishing programs and policies for church organization, maintaining the educational programs, supporting

ministry and mission. Through control of the formal
structure, some areas of responsibility and accountability
can be ignored and omitted from an organization's life.
(Most frequently, areas of ministry and mission are elim-
inated from the structure of church organizations.)

Structure also sets the context and limits for human
relationships. It makes possible and probable that some
people will interact and that other people will not have
any relationships of consequence for them or their concerns. People are placed at different distances from one
another through the structure of an organization. Through
this phenomenon a variety of expectations is created or
destroyed. Persons with ideas, commitments, and energy
have expectations of sharing these, and then discover that
they do not have access through regular channels to
share their gifts. Frequently these people become discour-
aged, frustrated, and drop out.

Occasionally informal structures are created through
the development of interest groups, study groups, or mission groups which then attempt to influence persons in
the formal structures. Sometimes this is successful and
the resources of persons are utilized. But all too often
these persons are viewed as an actual or potential threat
by those in the formal structure, the elite, and attempts
are made either to destroy the informal structures or to
render them ineffective or harmless. This really occurs,
this destruction of persons and their resources. This creation of powerlessness of persons to influence even their
own life of worship and service in churches is created
and maintained by those who rule and lead.

Structure, then, is one of the powerful factors in the
motivation of persons. Persons are motivated, committed,

and willing to share freely when their expectations have some possibility of fulfillment. Persons having access to the structures and the means through which their hopes can be fulfilled are motivated to work for the fulfillment of these hopes. When access is denied, there is little motivation to work only to fulfill the hopes, self-interest, and ideas of others. When a structure is created that is open and persons have access so that their diversity of ideas, commitments, and hopes can be shared, the whole organization becomes more active, vibrant, expectant, and a much higher level of energy and commitment becomes available to pursue tasks, goals, and purposes. When the only energy and resources available are from the minister and/or an elite group of laymen, or the top level of a church bureaucracy, the only meaningful resources available are from these few persons. Under such circumstances, a natural tendency toward organizational death proceeds in a relentless manner, and neither the minister nor the elite can stop the process unless they are willing to allow transformation of the structure and their relationships to persons in the organization.

There is a greater complexity to human organizations than most discussions about structure take into account. More is involved than simply the opposition of formal and informal structures. The motivations, thoughts, expectations, self-images, commitments, values, of people are involved—humans are involved—and they bring factors that make discussions of structure both more complex and more interesting.

Processes: The Means to Life

Structures define, set limits, and create settings in which relationships take place. The study of processes reveals most clearly how *power* is distributed within an organization, and how it is used. The processes of communication, decision-making, and patterns of interaction between people are expressions of values, interests, and theological commitments.

Power is certainly involved in communication. In most churches, communication processes and the media of communication are controlled by a small group so that only their messages are sent. For example, in one city recently the Council of Churches voted to ask all churches to sign a Good Neighbor pledge on a certain Sunday. One minister and his highest lay officer strongly opposed the idea, so cards were not placed in the pews and members of the congregation had no opportunity to choose to sign or not to sign. Pious sentiments may place barriers to our understanding and our appreciating this aspect of corporate church life, but nevertheless power is involved in all human communication.

When power is located in an individual or a group that has access to and control of meaningful rewards and punishments so that messages can be enforced, communication is relatively easy. (Example: when parents can give or take away meaningful rewards or punishments to children or adolescents, messages that the parents want them to hear and act upon can be enforced. If no meaningful rewards or punishments are available, or if parents do not have access to ones that are, parents may end up talking to themselves.) When there is disparity between the aims, goals, purposes, and mission of the ruling group and those whom they wish to do their bidding, power to enforce through the use of rewards and punishments is essential.

Few persons or groups have meaningful enforcing power in church organizations, but many would-be communicators act as if they do, or attempt to communicate through a one-way style that presupposes such power for effectiveness. But in an organization where coercive, enforcing power is not available (or desirable) to support communication, then one-way communication is difficult, if not impossible. Much preaching and teaching is not heard because of the lack of power in churches. Both ministers and laymen lack power to communicate. They cannot influence one another, and refuse to receive messages from one another. Through denying power to the other, through the attempt to contract and consolidate power, they lose power to communicate.

Much of communications theory in the church is based upon an outmoded understanding of power: that power is present only in static, given amounts in organizations and the elite must have as much of it as possible to communicate, control, and rule. In opposition to this is the idea that power is expandable. If someone gains power, others do not necessarily lose power. Through expanding the amount of power available in an organization, every person gains some. (See Amitai Etzioni, *The Active Society,* pp. 313–381; The Free Press, 1968.)

In communication, in decision-making, or in group interaction, the easier it is for *all* groups in an organization to have their messages heard, to actually have the power to send messages and have them openly received by other groups, including ruling, elite groups, the better the organization functions. All groups, including ruling groups, have more power to communicate and, hence, greater capacity to influence decisions and more willingness to act on those decisions. One of the tragedies of our time is that we do not work to make one another powerful. We cling to the vestiges of power that remain from our attempts to control, to preserve, and to maintain that little power remaining, rather than explore the ways in which all can receive and handle more power.

Power is involved in all processes of church organizations. It is a crucial issue in the sickness or health of these organizations. The issue is not whether Christians are involved in power, but which understanding of power we have and what judges, directs, and informs this understanding and use of power in interaction, communication, and decision-making.

Power, as suggested earlier, is involved in the alienation of persons. As power expands, with more people receiving more of it, the possibility of the enhancement of reconciliation and the overcoming of alienation occurs. There is never reconciliation between unequals, between the powerful and the powerless. True reconciliation occurs only between equals. We have the possibility of being reconciled when we are both powerful, when we can influence one another, when we can share our messages, our gifts, our faith commitments, and our energy with one another.

This is true in the church school classroom where a group of pupils is alienated from the teacher who cannot listen, who will not alter plans for the class, or who sees herself as the only authority. The class thwarts or sits in silence, resenting every moment of the period. The class exercises its limited power by reducing the teacher to a state of powerlessness. She cannot communicate the lesson. Power is negative and contracting, rather than positive and expanding. Tasks, purposes, and mission all suffer under these circumstances.

The condition described in this church school class can be duplicated in most church organizations where formal processes of communication, interaction, and decision-making alienate people through a faulty understanding of power. In most alienating situations, persons have only negative power, which they use through informal communication channels. They attempt in numerous ways to thwart the persons who rule and the decisions made by these persons. In any organization where people cannot influence the decision-making processes, where they are powerless to help in creating the conditions under which they will live and share their gifts, alienation occurs and the whole body suffers. In fact, there can be no whole body where the separate members cannot contribute to the whole that which is uniquely theirs to share.

The processes of organization life are the ways in which the body of Christ functions. Power, alienation, and reconciliation are involved in these processes. Communication, decision-making, and interaction in our organizations need to be informed and qualified by our commitments as Christians.

CONTENT: THE DIRECTION OF LIFE

Most church organizations are known for their formal content, theology, which is contained in the pronounce-

ments, confessions of faith, curricular resources, and statements of ministry and mission. The most nonfunctional
aspects of any organization are these formal statements.
Formal structures and processes do their work of setting
the context for tasks and persons and defining functions
and relationships. Formal theological positions, except in
rare organizations, have little to do with any aspect of
formal organizational life except filling space in liturgy.
They are nonfunctional in that they do not inform, judge,
or direct the organization's life. There is little, if any,
correlation between the theology contained in our confessions and curricular resources and preaching, committee life, and our organizational understanding of mission
and ministry.

Informal values, ideology, and theological commitments are the source of direction for most organizations.
In the church, this informal content ranges from definitions of Christianity as an American cultural religion in
which the major commitments may be to God, democracy,
and "doing good in the world," to that peculiar American
expression of pietistic fundamentalism—belief in the Bible,
God, and doing good individually. This may appear to be
a superficial characterization. It is not meant to be that,
since much of Christianity is this vague and meaningless.
Granted, there are significant minorities in the church who
gravitate toward these extremes but who are thoughtful,
serious, and honest in their beliefs. But the point here is
that no matter what these informal beliefs may be, they
do not generally function to judge, direct, and inform
the life of Christians in the institutional church.

It is as though the institutional church existed apart
from the faith commitments of its rhetoric. Most Amer-

ican theology that is functional in the life of the church people is too individualistic to be appropriate for the creation of a living body of Christ. This is true even though we recognize the centrality of the ideas "people of God," "church," and "body of Christ" in Scripture. Scripture does not inform our corporate, institutional life.

The direction of church organizational life ought to be found in the formal theological commitments of a people. Church organizational life, in every aspect of its being, is a creation and expression of men. This creation needs to be subject to that which transcends it, the Word of God become flesh, Jesus Christ. Thus far, our formal theological positions have little to do with either the formal or informal aspects of church life. Structures, leadership styles, communication patterns, and relationships are not informed by our theological confessions and stances. We meet as denominational groups, adopt confessions, and forget them. They do not speak to how we run our churches, how we order worship, how we engage in ministry and mission. They are forgotten documents except when we repeat them in unison during worship.

The reason for this, I am sure, is that we are a people, clergy and laity, who are not really serious about our life as the church. It does not seem, in its present condition, to be a source of hope and life to us. If we were serious, we would work for that perspective, mutually, which would inform our common life. Ministers and laity would work together to discern the relationships between confessions of faith and the concrete life of the church. Much of preaching and teaching is without direction because churchmen do not see any significant relation between preaching-teaching, curricula, and confessions. When we

are without direction, when our formal theological
stances do not inform us, we preach and teach whatever
comes to mind—the latest theological fad, the most contemporary social issue, or tradition and the Bible as we
received it. What is needed for most churchmen is a framework for understanding and guiding our thoughts and
actions, whether they be preaching-teaching, counseling,
decision-making on governing boards, or the development
of resources and strategies by denominational boards
and agencies. Most of us are victims of the moment, and
in that moment we do not function as churchmen with a
perspective (values, ideology, theology) that frees us
and enables us to meet present situations more appropriately as Christians and more effectively as churchmen.
Too frequently, we are overwhelmed by present dissen-
sion, crises, and problems because we lack a perspective
on life and work.

An understanding of our everyday life as the body of
Christ, which is also a missionary body, ought to provide
us with such a perspective. Our structures, processes of
interaction and communication, and the formal theological content (our confessions, preaching-teaching, and
curricular resources) need to be informed by such a self-
understanding. Every aspect of our organizational life
ought to be a witness (and in fact this life *is* a witness to
something) to our being God's people. No structures, no
arrangements of people in time and space, are necessarily
"Christian." The church of New Testament times had
many structural forms. But there are forms that can en-
hance and promote reconciliation, love and justice, care
for persons, communication, ministry, and mission.

Love and justice expressed in the structures of the

church are the necessary conditions for continuing growth as the body of Christ. Justice for liberals, conservatives, men, women, adolescents, and children is essential in the body of Christ so that *no one* is powerless in Christian faith, so that everyone knows who he is in the church. There can be no reconciliation, and there is neither love nor justice, when people who have different knowledge, interests, and competencies in the church do not know themselves as persons who are valued because they have these gifts to share. To know oneself as a person who has some gifts to share, who is an authentic member of that interdependent body of Christ, and who has the power to share his gifts with other members of the body is a central and crucial aspect of reconciliation.

Power to contribute, to share, to be involved meaningfully; justice in structures, communication, and decision-making processes; love in relationships; and self-understanding as a genuine contributing member of an organic body are the elements of reconciliation and the true sign that the institutional church as the body of Christ has as its head Jesus of Nazareth. When these elements are present in the body, in the institutional church, churchmen and the world have no need to look for anything better. They have a source of hope.

A postscript is necessary to emphasize one point. In order for the institution to be an expression of Christian faith there must be justice for all. No exceptions! Without justice (as described by Isaiah, Hosea, and Amos) in our organizational life, whether family, local church, board, or agency, there is no love, no power, no self-understanding as a worthwhile member, no reconciliation—no body of Christ!

With a grasp of the direction of a people as the body of Christ, structures, processes, and theological directives can be created by the people to express this reality. This institutional creation can never be a pure expression of the body of Christ. It *can* be a proximate expression based upon the commitments, understanding, and energy of a people living in a particular moment. It should be apparent by now that no aspect of institutional church life is neutral, of no consequence, for persons in the organization.

The most significant factor in organizational life is that which points the direction and informs every facet of the institution. For this reason clergy and laity together must theologize, must think as Christians, using the sources for thinking that are available to them—Scripture, tradition, formal theology, confessions of faith, experience, and the world with its knowledge. Direction for our life as the church comes from all these sources. The perspective for shaping structures, processes, and a variety of contents that are more or less appropriate expressions of Christian faith comes from people thinking as Christians in their situation, using the sources available to them.

Organizations, including church organizations, are more than what those purveyors of organizational charts think they are. There is more to reforming organizations than changing structure, drawing new charts in which men are rearranged in their boxes to do their appointed tasks. All organizations are living, dynamic, complex entities in which people are feeling, thinking, thwarting, protecting self-interests, and promoting economic and political goals. Any organization can be understood, at least partially, through looking at its structures, processes, and contents. In church organizations, these structures, processes, and contents are the forms through which Christian faith is expressed. The forms are extensions of ourselves and our commitments.

To recognize the church as the body of Christ places a mandate before churchmen to become persons committed to the role of agents of change for the institutional church. They will see themselves as agents of change who will dare to struggle with new or transformed structures for caring for the church and the world. They will seek new or transformed processes for communication, decision-making, and interaction through which the gifts of all members can be received, appreciated, and shared both within the church and without. Most important, they will be agents who will try to discover appropriate theological expressions to support and maintain the life of the body of Christ in ministry and mission.

But are we qualified to do that?

8

CLERGY AND LAITY—
AGENTS OF INSTITUTIONAL
CHANGE

> Let no one disqualify you insisting on self-abasement and worship of angels, taking his stand on visions, puffed up without reason by his sensuous mind, and not holding fast to the Head, from whom the whole body, nourished and knit together through its joints and ligaments, grows with a growth that is from God. (Col. 2:18-19.)

Growth means change. There is no growth without change in relationships, functions, and purposes. But as growth occurs in the human body, this change is never revolutionary except when extreme illness occurs, as in malignant tumors when cells grow wildly, forgetting relationships, functions, and purposes. Rather, there is a continual transformation of the various interdependent systems. There is never a moment when change is not occurring in living organisms.

The imagery of the writer of Colossians suggests that the same change or transforming processes ought to characterize the collective life of Christians. The church grows and changes continuously as it commits itself to become the body of Christ. And the nature and direction of change is qualified, directed, and judged as the body holds "fast to the Head," Jesus Christ who is from God.

The head of the body remains constant. But the joints and ligaments need to be examined and encouraged to grow. These joints and ligaments in church organizations are the structures, the decision-making, communication, and interaction processes, and the theological contents we provide for one another. Change in them should be made for the purpose of more appropriately expressing Christian faith. For, as we have already discussed, we express our faith not only through preaching-teaching and liturgy, but also through the mundane parts of the institution—in committee meetings, church school classes, or times of fellowship.

The ministry of clergy and laity is the same as the ministry of Jesus Christ: caring for God's people gathered and in the world. But a dramatic shift in the focus of ministry is called for—from a selective focus upon individuals as the object of ministry to a new focus on the church organizations. Appropriate ministry to church organizations must be thought of in wider terms than merely preaching, pastoral care, church worship attendance, and raising the annual budget. Church services can be well attended, hundreds of pastoral calls can be made, and the annual budget can be oversubscribed, and the body of Christ may still be a nonfunctioning collection of individuals who care adequately neither for themselves and their fellow members nor for the world. Another dimension must be added to the traditional ministry of clergy and laity: the ministry to the institution in order that it can *be* that body of Christ which changes and grows in its capacity to provide ministries for itself and the world.

Few clergy and laity know and understand organizations. Fewer still possess knowledge and skill with which to develop health and effectiveness in them. At this moment the church is desperately in need of persons who can work with people to bring about continual transformation.

We referred earlier to "agents of change." This term needs clarification. Persons are needed in our institutions who do not seek personal power and influence, but organizational effectiveness in developing ministries within the institutional church and between that church and the institutions of society. "Change agents" are needed who are committed to developing an organization that accomplishes its purposes, and who are concerned to use the contributions of others throughout the whole organization for the sake of its ministries, purposes, and goals. As laymen sit on governing boards they must care sufficiently for the institutional church to change it so that it sets priorities, directions, and meaningful objectives—and then develop the *organizational* means for achieving them.

In every human organization we are political creatures. The church is no exception. We nominate, elect, control decisions through a variety of means, develop personal relationships so that we influence people, and use techniques of public relations to create images that people will support. Suggesting that church life is political does not mean that it is evil and to be avoided, or that we can be a church and not be political. We are and must be political. To be human means to be political. It is not possible to deny our humanity as we are churchmen. We are called, in fact, to be human and to be churchmen.

The question is not whether the church organization is political, but what should direct, guide, and judge its political life. A concept of ourselves as the body of Christ, commissioned to minister both to ourselves and to others? Or commitment to maintenance of vested interests and an institution per se? The former makes growth or change an essential character of corporate life. The latter promotes stagnation, defensiveness, and eventual death as the church. There can be no living church without change as a continuous feature.

In too many church organizations clergy and laity are politically power-oriented. They imagine themselves to be agents of change, but their primary concern is not growth and change as the body of Christ but control of people, programs, money, membership, and direction through political processes. They use a variety of means to get a majority vote on issues in local churches, judicatories, or boards and agencies. If it is not possible to get such a vote, then effort is made to get the same result without referendum. Composition of nominating committees is controlled so that only persons who agree with the existing leadership and who will nominate like-minded persons are appointed to the committee.

Both clergy and laity are guilty of using these devices. Conservatives and liberals use the same techniques and strategies to maintain their control of present structures and decision-making processes that are effective in protecting their interest. Considerable energy and power—political, economic, and social—are used by a few to maintain their own interests. When this occurs, there is injustice, inequality, powerlessness, and polarization. The result is maximum conditions for thwarting or revolt and low motivation for involvement of the many in the programs of the few.

This political style (employed by both liberal and conservative leadership) promotes alienation. No theological critique is brought to bear upon such political life. The old argument that the end justifies the means is proffered. We look at the residue of feudalism and nineteenth-century leadership styles in society and conclude that church leadership must act in the same manner.

What exists in society should never be considered as normative for church leaders. The action of power elites in segments of society is not sufficient reason for adopting this style of leadership for the church without fundamental theological criticism. The life of church organizations as an expression of Christian faith is the only worthy end and goal of church leadership.

But those who consider themselves change agents in many church organizations reject or ignore this end—which is one of the ministries of Jesus Christ—and actually create polarization, disruption, alienation, and paralysis through their political style. Liberals who are change agents decry the rugged individualism, the elitism, the unresponsiveness, and the nineteenth-century assumptions of conservatives. The irony is that liberals, when in power, exhibit the same political style and the same assumptions, and the same end result occurs—a sick organization. It does not make any difference, as far as the health of an organization is concerned, whether liberals or conservatives rule if neither is judged or directed by an understanding of faith that provides a critique of the political life of the church.

Meanwhile, a more contemporary political style is

emerging in many secular organizations. This style emphasizes the processes of decision-making within organizations, opening these processes to all persons and groups who have interests, knowledge, and competencies to share in the consideration of particular issues and problems. Innovation, expression of multiple interests and concerns, and a variety of purposes are appreciated. Rather than a static group in continuous rule, divergent groups form and re-form to exert leadership around problems and issues of the moment.

In contrast to the church's current political style, which assumes that the interests of those few making the decision represent the range of interests of the entire congregation and that sufficient knowledge and skill are present among the few to accomplish the congregation's tasks, this new style maintains that interests, knowledge, and competencies are to be found in multiple places. This means that rather than a single ruling group there are multiple groups that take part in rule. Minorities' rule, rather than *a* minority rule, exists. Authority is lodged among various groups, and responsibility and accountability are extended throughout the organization rather than remaining in the hands of a few. The resources of the whole body become available. This new style may seem utopian, but among those organizations which have adopted it, healthiness and effectiveness in accomplishing missions is sure evidence of its viability.

Gathering the best expertise is a central function of the change agent within a church that sees itself as a diversified, unified body of Christ. In the past we have had too little concern for expertise, knowledge, and competency. We likewise have ignored the multiple interests of people around issues and problems. Most decision-making is informed only by the interest of the few at the top. Far more attention needs to be given to building into the decision-making processes the multiple interests and the available knowledge and competencies from wherever they are located in a church organization. This means that governing boards will search throughout the church for the best people to help make decisions, rather than the persons who are in the traditional leadership positions. Decisions will become informed, programs will be manned, and strategies will be developed by the most well-equipped persons, the most interested persons, and the most knowledgeable persons.

In this new style of leadership there is an equalization of power as dynamic interaction between individuals and groups takes place. Interdependency is encouraged as individuals and groups share what they possess. Conflicts, tensions, and differences become realities that are dealt with as sources of creativity, motivation, and energy for growth. The management of conflict—not smothering, ignoring, or burying it—is one of those skills necessary for the enhancement of political life.

The change agent in a church organization is a political person in a political organization. Too long we have hidden this political activity and the styles it represents behind spiritual rhetoric, clerical garbs, and sentimentalism. If we care sufficiently about the church and its calling to be the body of Christ, we will make all our life as visible as possible, including our political life and the political activity of our leaders, and bring this life under the scrutiny of faith commitments.

One task of a change agent is to help persons become

honest about life in their organizations, and to help these persons discover the resources already there that can bring health to the organizations. The prerequisite for health is an accurate diagnosis of the causes of illness, and then a marshaling of the resources for combating the disease. Therapy from outside is designed to aid the functioning elements already working in the body.

Many persons who imagine themselves to be change agents are successful at gathering clusters of like-minded persons around them. Both conservatives and liberals have their ingroups. Both listen to their own rhetoric and dismiss the arguments and programs of others. Too frequently, self-righteousness characterizes both groups. Rather than commit themselves to the labor of changing political styles and transforming decision-making and communication processes (including their own), they harden the lines. They become one of the causes of illness.

True agents of change need to develop skills for lifting up differences and creating a climate in which persons can deal with differences honestly. No more dishonesty in committees! Too many laymen and clergy sit silently on committees hiding their feelings and ideas. There is too much waste in church organizational life that is seen in just plain boredom with what is going on. And leadership that is insecure or defensive doesn't care to discover the reason why people feel that nothing is at stake in church meeting after church meeting. Time, energy, ideas, and skills are wasted on a fantastic scale.

A political style that encourages persons with differences to care enough to become involved offers the means for best fulfilling our understanding of ourselves as the body of Christ. *No political style is Christian.* The question that change agents need to answer is: Which political style creates the conditions most favorable to the expression of Christian faith?

One style we have already seen to be ineffective—control from the top by a few. Frequently we have thought that something has been accomplished when a vote has been taken and a successful outcome has resulted in a pronouncement, or a strategy, or a program approval. Months later when evaluation takes place, we discover that nothing has happened. No change has taken place— no one has acted on the pronouncement, and programs are unformed or unsupported.

Organizational change consists of something more than ramming a program, or a pronouncement, or a strategy through an organization to a successful vote. Change means change in structures, processes, and theological commitments. Changing these requires that the people who are currently in the organization change them. No power play is really successful. Thwarting, backlash, revolt, and alienation are the inevitable end results.

Revolutionary change in the institutions of most societies is extremely difficult under the most advantageous circumstances. In a middle-class, educated society, change can take place only in cooperation with the persons involved. This means transformation rather than revolution. People who are affected by change must change their organization, and in a sense themselves, if change is to be more than gesture or pronouncement.

Persons who want to be effective in changing organizations must work with people and information to effect change. The style of working that people will accept, respect, and respond to is currently changing. The people dimension of change is altering dramatically. The conditions under which leaders can arbitrarily be authoritative change agents no longer exist. Knowledge and competency have become essential attributes for change agents, coupled with an ability to hear and act upon the interests and concerns of others, and to utilize the knowledge and skills of other persons. Change agents alone cannot change organizations, but must depend for their effectiveness upon their ability to work with persons mutually creating new conditions, objectives, and strategies.

The information dimension of organizational life has changed as well. No person has access to all the relevant data for decision-making. The effective change agent is the one who enables persons in an organization to seek better, more accurate information upon which to base decisions. This means that persons and groups who have information must be sought and encouraged to share what they know. Through commitment by an organization to act upon the best information available, dependence upon one-man or one-group rule is minimized.

The person who seeks to effect change solely through personal political power, through the power of position and the power of influence of personal relationships with friends of long standing, is in trouble today. The changes in expectations, self-understanding, and values of people, and the explosion of knowledge render him increasingly ineffective and defensive. Young Turks rise up and challenge this style of leadership. Members boycott annual meetings, governing-board sessions, and committee meetings. In the background we hear the noise of people complaining about insensitive and incompetent leadership.

Both organizations and styles of transforming them are in need of changing. Processes for changing and for equipping persons involved in the processes need updating, or the present anti-institutionalism in the church will be only a prelude to complete lack of confidence, meaning, and consequence in the lives of both individuals and society.

Growth, change, in church organizations is brought about primarily through administration and education. These are profound institutional activities. Clergy and laity alike have misunderstood the significance of these activities in effecting change. The manner in which lay leaders help committees to focus upon objectives, plan strategies, seek and use all the information available, and evaluate effectiveness of programs in existence are change activities. Every committee that has a climate of openness, honesty, and a style of working expressive of Christian faith is a source of hope to every other committee. Education that equips laity and clergy for effective life in which growth results in the organization is part of changing that organization.

Change in its style of operation, however, will not come without cost. The psychological and physical costs are great to change agents who help a church organization to develop a new political style, a new climate, new structures, processes, and theological contents. Change comes through their commitment to be involved in changing the organization, to be personally involved in caring for it, and to be willing to share whatever they have in promoting health. Courage, sensitivity to people and their concerns, skills in stepping into conflicts and helping to manage them, and the ability to recognize, use, and rely upon the gifts of others are essential requisites for a change agent. The temptation for most change agents is to manipulate people and processes in an attempt to predetermine the end. It takes great commitment to discipline oneself to trust people and a process that one can't control and to believe that the products of a political style that is nonmanipulative can produce a superior solution, program, or idea.

Political activity enhances growth and change within the body of Christ or it thwarts transformation. In political church life, where a variety of groups can be powerful, there is a built-in capacity to respond to challenges and an ability to innovate, to create new conditions, new ministries, new relationships, and new structures that are expressive of Christian faith. But growth is possible only where conditions of justice and love prevail, where reconciliation is possible. Political styles determine the preconditions under which faith finds expression. Where structures are rigid and decision-making processes are closed, neither justice nor love can prevail, and reconciliation is impossible. We do not have a choice as to whether we will be political or apolitical in church organizations. We do have control over the direction our politics will take.

The ministry of institutional change has been largely ignored. Few clergy and laity are equipped to change organizations, and few genuinely appreciate that church organizations need continuous transformation. The elite of most church organizations resist change rather than promote growth of the organization to the end that its life reflects the faith commitments, resources, and energy of the whole body.

But clergy and laity together must be agents of institutional change if our perspective and activity are governed by Christian faith. Changing church and secular organizations is a theological activity. We change not for the sake of change, or to be contemporary, or to implement the latest fads, no matter whether they be educational, liturgical, or "mission" expressions. Our only valid basis for changing is to live our lives as the body of Christ.

9

TRANSFORMING CHURCH ORGANIZATIONS

One congregation is located in the middle of one of the fastest-changing neighborhoods in the country. Real estate speculators are purchasing every house and apartment building available to convert into apartments for young professionals who can pay high rents. Families are moving from the area to suburbs where housing is available and less expensive. Urban renewal is removing families and the poor. With the removal of white families, the area high school has been thrown into a turmoil. A high school integrated since the turn of the century has suddenly developed into a typical ghetto high school. Disturbances, tensions, and fear characterize the school. Housing for the elderly has been constructed that will concentrate hundreds of older persons in the community. Young people are on pot and other more potent drugs. Groups of adolescents wander the streets and stake out claims for their own turf.

This congregation lives tensely in the middle of such changes, unsure of itself. There are some members who remember the days of fewer challenges and problems. Yet amid all the changes this congregation remains healthy. It has committed itself to a positive response to the new conditions. Objectives have been developed. Debate has been an essential component of the process of setting these objectives in a statement of ministry for the whole congregation. Every committee and group has discussed, modified, and examined its own objectives and programs in the light of the direction set by the entire congregation. The annual meeting where the statement of ministry is examined, debated, changed, and adopted has become the liveliest, most vital meeting of the congregation. Every aspect of congregational life is included in the concerns of the congregation: worship, education, community, the elderly, youth, and schools. This congregation understands itself as a community of ministries. Not all members agree that every ministry is valid or important, but there is a willingness to bless the ministry of others. This congregation is characterized by its ability to use many of the resources of its members in a variety of ministries.

Contrast this congregation to one in a small town where community leaders attend worship only occasionally and the highest-quality contribution to the life of the congregation is consistently made by the choir. Young people have deserted the church. Delinquency is high in the community. Use of alcohol and drugs creates major problems. Unemployment is high. The most enlightened, aggressive young leaders have moved away, leaving behind those who are least equipped to deal with the problems of a dying community. Businessmen are conservative and defensive, unable to cope with new patterns of merchandising, business, and industry. Schools are not supported by an adequate tax base or an understanding community and school board. Poverty of people, money, ideas, and programs surrounds the church in this community. Change is taking place. Outsiders—businessmen and educators—come into the community occasionally to upset the patterns. But because no one is equipped to meet the changes, most of the consequences of change are negative for both the church and the community. Only the church school and the women's organization exist to respond to the challenge facing this congregation.

Another congregation is located in an affluent suburb. Hundreds of young families move in and out of the community every year. Many of these young adults are gifted, educated, and concerned, but are unable to find an outlet for their concerns and their knowledge in the congregation to which they belong. A five-year period of membership is required before a person is eligible to be elected to the governing board. No avenues are open for evaluating current ministries or for developing new ones. Tension and frustration exist throughout the congregation. Small groups of concerned persons have met to discuss topics ranging from How do we get rid of the present clergy staff? or How can we influence the governing board? to Is there another church in the community that will take our concerns seriously? Some members of the congregation have already taken their membership elsewhere. Others have made the League of Women Voters or the local human relations committee their church. Still others have dropped out of sight. They will emerge again to try the next minister.

This congregation exists in a community where the problems are fantastic. Drug use by the affluent adolescents is increasing. Marriages and families are in desper-

ate need of help. Problems abound in the local schools.
Most of the men work in the city and many are concerned
about its overwhelming problems. They need and desire
help in understanding their ministry and the ministry
of their industry in the city. They want the congregation
to be involved and supportive. But this congregation is
governed by local businessmen who have grown up in the
community and who lack that broader exposure and
equipment to deal with the problems of both the church
and the community which is required today. Most of
these leaders resist adult education in the congregation,
especially for themselves.

The question facing each of these congregations is:
What are the ministries that ought to characterize our life
as the body of Christ? Or, in Moltmann's words, what is
the "other institution" in which there is hope because persons and groups are concerned with that which is "true,
eternal life, the true and eternal dignity of man, true and
just relationships"? All our organizations need changing.
How do we proceed?

DETERMINING DIRECTION

Growth depends upon the ability of persons to focus
upon the variety of ministries, and the objectives, priorities, and commitments that are appropriate manifesta-
tions of the body of Christ. There can be no meaningful
change that is expressive of Christian faith unless there is
selective, disciplined focusing upon the goals of the organization. Governing boards, executive committees,
staffs, committees, task forces, in fact every group in an
organization, need to search for the objectives of the

whole organization, and the interdependent, necessary relation between a particular group and the other parts. For example, if the nature and meaning of worship is a problem to the congregation, then governing boards, women's groups, youth groups, men's organizations, and the church school must be involved in focusing upon this problem. Worship is a function of the whole congregation. No small committee or pastor can revitalize worship independently of other groups.

Every organization and age group within a congregation needs to be involved in discussing and deciding the ministries necessary if the church is to exist as the body of Christ, caring for itself and the world. Persons who are cared for must be part of the process of deciding the nature and form of caring. The decisions of the various groups should be written so that the whole congregation understands and subscribes to the variety of ministries that characterize the life of the people. In a changing world and in rapidly changing communities these objectives, goals, and ministries need continual criticism and evaluation.

Agents of change ought to guide the processes of development of such a statement and enable groups to focus upon their understanding of the objectives and priorities. They do this best by making information and people with faith commitments, skills, and knowledge available. They also help to develop the procedures for criticism and evaluation of current ideas, programs, and ministries.

DIAGNOSING FOR CHANGE

Change takes place in a variety of places, at different speeds, beginning with individuals, groups, committees, and segments of an organization most eager to change. Effective leadership first diagnoses where the greatest readiness and capacity exists to carry out the commitments and priorities of the organization. The organization is carefully studied to determine the persons and groups with ideas that are ready to attempt new ministries, to evaluate current programming, and to work as a task force on a new problem.

Next, an inventory is made of persons within the organization and the skills and knowledge of those persons available to work on the priorities of the organization. Knowledge of an organization and its capabilities is a crucial part of changing. We depend too much on the traditional leadership of the church. We exhaust our known resources because we have not developed what is there but unknown. Too frequently, leadership waits for the "right" persons rather than developing the persons and resources already in the organization. One of the favorite and most ineffective ways of changing an organization is to play musical chairs with persons—transfer them from committee to committee, from job to job, hoping to discover the correct combination. We rarely intentionally develop the capabilities and capacities of the persons we have. In fact, we rarely know what the gifts are that people can share.

A third step in diagnosis for change takes place when we look to see what is changeable and then discover the persons best equipped to contribute to transforming that program, ministry, or issue. Change, again, does not always depend upon the traditional leadership located in the standard positions. Persons are found throughout the organization who can best lead, depending upon what is needed. Through this understanding of leadership, we not only increase the ability of the organization to change, we also develop a style of working together in an organization that increases the values of persons, enhances reconciliation, and encourages collaboration of persons for the welfare of the whole body.

CREATING STRUCTURES TO SERVE GOALS

When leadership is understood as utilization of the persons best equipped to carry forward the priorities of the people, the traditional understanding of power is altered. There is increased mutuality, greater involvement in decision-making, and power is located throughout the organization. Decision-making processes and structures exist for implementing the objectives, goals, and ministries of the organization. Structures are created to bring together the persons and resources needed for the variety of ministries. No organization can cope with the challenges of today with an unchanged structure. Nor will a new structure continue to be "good" to carry out the organization's purposes for years to come. Structures are created to serve objectives and goals.

Two functions need to be kept in mind as structures are designed. First, persons and resources need to be brought together for acting on commitments in particular areas. Concentration and specialization are necessary for maximum response to challenges. Second, there needs to be a binding together, an integration function, between the various parts. The eye functions both alone, to see, and in connection with the hand that needs to pick up a pen. The foot supports the body alone, but moves only in communication with the leg. These two functions—specialization and integration—need to exist in every organization if it is to be healthy.

It is easy to think too narrowly about the resources from which we can draw. We often not only fail to tap what is available within organizations, but also are unaware that more resources than we can ever use exist outside our organizations in other local churches, judicatories, boards and agencies, seminaries, universities, and governmental units. Structures need to be created which will bring a variety of resources together that will inform and support the ministries of church organizations.

In a day when it is almost unchristian to be antiecumenical, there needs to be honesty about ecumenical organizations. In some communities ecumenical structures may serve the best means for developing ministries both within and without local congregations. In other communities, or for particular problems in a community, resources, commitments, and knowledge may be lacking, so that ecumenical structures would only destroy or cause ineffective ministries to be developed. There needs to be maximum freedom to develop structures that use available resources and promote ministry. We need to make the same critical, diagnostic appraisal of ecumenical groups that we make of other organizations and to judge cooperation between denominations with the same theological perspective we use within our own denomination.

As members of the body of Christ, when is it most helpful to the whole body for us to cooperate? When is it harmful or unnecessary?

Effective ecumenical ministry at any level depends upon healthy local organizations. The ministries of ecumenical groups need the widest possible support from local organizations. No ministry can occur without persons engaging in these ministries. Official hierarchy and clergy involvement in ecumenical structures is not sufficient for ministry. It is true that more resources are available, larger and more effective strategies are possible, with significant ecumenical involvement, but this hinges on the health and effectiveness of the various organizations.

We develop structures for the sake of our goals as the body of Christ. The criteria of appropriateness and effectiveness of ministries must be the same for all structures. It is our ministry that expresses our life as the body of Christ. Structure, hopefully, is a means to the expression of that ministry.

COMMUNICATIONS FOR CHANGING

Most thought about communications in church organizations is on a superficial level. We attempt unprofessional public-relations approaches, newsletters, and memo methods. In changing church organizations, an effective human communications network is needed in which everything is open. Honesty must be evident in every aspect of the decision-making processes. Communication requires a two-directional flow. Not only must the life of the organization be open and easily read, but also feedback consisting of the attitudes, opinions, and ideas about that life must be received and acted upon. Changing depends upon persons trusting and understanding the messages and those who send messages. Change agents must work on the honesty and clarity of messages, and the response to those messages by those who develop ministries.

LEADERSHIP FOR CHANGING

Organizations that intend to change must develop leaders who can be change agents. Much of present leadership development in the church is abstract, and functions to perpetuate paralysis. The church can no longer afford to have leadership development programs in and of themselves.

Development of leaders must be for organizational growth, for developing structures, processes, and theological contents to reach specific goals. Education of change agents for specific organizational tasks, for governing boards, for specific community ministries, and for particular tasks in educational ministries must occur. Change occurs only when persons have faith commitments which they must act upon and when these persons are equipped to change the groups and committees with which they work most intimately. The personality, character, or climate of the body is changed by beginning with particular groups that either are engaged in ministry to the congregation or are part of the organization's ministry to the community.

Leaders of groups need to know how to help members attack problems and issues confronting them. In the past we have not taught laity how to approach educational problems of the congregation, issues in the community, or problems of caring for members of the congregation. Neither clergy nor laity know intuitively the best means for developing ministries to the elderly, youth groups, schools, single young adults, or the poor. A variety of structures, of decision-making, communication, and interaction processes, and of theological reflections is necessary for these ministries.

We also need to sort out the types of leadership needed by organizations for different tasks, and then to develop persons for the tasks they do best. Some persons function well in organizational maintenance roles—caring for buildings, raising budgets, organizing and servicing the traditional and necessary tasks. Other persons are better equipped to develop new ministries, ideas, and programs. Both need to be freed to contribute their abilities. Each is essential if an organization is to be healthy and effective. Frequently we mismatch, placing creative persons in maintenance roles and maintenance persons in creative roles. The result is frustration for the persons and the organization.

Another error we commit is to give authority to institutional maintenance persons for regulating and controlling creative ministries and program-oriented persons. These ministries need to function interdependently and cooperatively rather than independently or competitively. In changing organizations, leaders and groups have to be challenged by their tasks and given the freedom and support to do what they can.

Local churches are notorious for the competition and conflict that exist between those who care for property and those who are responsible for programming. New leadership development programs should take each kind of leadership seriously and attempt to develop leaders in both groups who can collaborate for the growth of the church. One of the criteria for the selection and development of leaders ought to be: Can they collaborate with people who disagree with them, so that the organization is free to change? If leaders cannot collaborate, there is little possibility for change. There is also a theological dimension to this problem. Coupled with the criterion mentioned above ought to be one that requires that leaders have a commitment to theological reflection about their leadership. Can they criticize their own style of leadership on the basis of their faith commitments?

Leadership education programs must begin to equip persons with knowledge and skills to help them engage in theological reflection about their organizational activities. In addition, prospective leaders need skills necessary for collaboration, for conflict management, and for helping others to share their ideas and skills. New people coming into organizations, turmoil in the community, challenges from people within the organization, and rebellion by constituency in judicatories require new understandings and new skills for leaders.

Most leaders in church organizations have not been equipped for the jobs they are doing. We can be grateful for the willingness of lay volunteers and clergy bureaucrats who, in spite of the tensions and frustrations inherent in the churches, continue to share what they have. This gratitude, however, relieves no one of the responsibility to equip leaders for the tasks they face today. Few are happy with the crises in the church. Most do not know how to handle them. We have been reluctant to think of the church as an organization that requires leadership to change its organizations. But if these organizations are to become even proximate expressions of Christian faith, our most important task today is experimentation in the development of leaders at every level of church organization who can help us through multiple crises.

THE TIMES OF GROWTH

In every organization there are three formal moments of transformation, moments when both individuals and organizations undergo change, if change takes place. These are not the only times of change. The culture or personality of an organization has its effect continuously. But these are times when every organization should concentrate on its own growth and the growth of individuals, and the goals, priorities, and ministries of the organization should be as visible as possible during these moments.

The time of incorporation of new persons is probably most important. During this period the climate or character of an organization needs to be lifted up so that entering persons can see it, understand it, and make the critical decision about the meaning of membership in the organization.

In local churches, most new-member classes are not incorporation processes. They are poor indoctrination. Lectures on the history of the church, history of the de-

nomination, contemporary theology, and how the local
church operates are not an interpretation of the local
church as a people engaged in a variety of ministries caring for themselves and the world as Christ's people. Incorporation means that persons become integrated, functioning members of a body that has direction, purposes,
and goals. Ways must be discovered for helping persons
to become functioning members as soon as possible. Part
of the process of incorporation ought to be a candid, open
discussion of the resources that a new member has and
how *he desires* to become a functioning member who
shares these resources for the sake of the whole body.
This means an in-depth exposure to the variety of ministries of the congregation so that new persons have a basis
for decision and an understanding of the commitments
of the congregation from experience. Incorporation is not
a function of clergy who give lectures, but of the whole
congregation, which extends the various facets of its life
to new members and makes this life available.

In a real sense the time of incorporation is the time of
justification of the life of committees and groups in a
congregation to new members and to themselves. It may
be a shock to some groups to discover that they have no
ministry. They are not doing the work of Jesus Christ and,
consequently, there is no reason for their existence as
members of the body of Christ. In fact they are *not* members, because they are not doing the work of the head.

All communicant members should be functioning members of congregations. Adolescents are the forgotten
Christians. They are full members by every formal criterion, but have no designated functions. Frankly, we
want their names on church rolls but often resent their

minds and bodies engaged in ministry. We offer few opportunities for ministry by which young people can be incorporated into the life of the church. Our indoctrination of them is even more obscure, boring, and irrelevant than it is for adults. Very seldom do we even attempt to describe what it means for the adolescent to be a churchman. We ask him to collect the offering, fold bulletins, paint walls, and other innocuous tasks, but we hold no challenge of ministry before him. It should not be a surprise that young people drop out of the church. They do not really drop out, because you cannot quit something to which you have never belonged. Few young people drop out of church when they are functioning members who are engaged in the variety of ministries of the congregation. The creativity, idealism, and energy of young persons is grossly wasted. We do not challenge them to contribute their interests, skills, and knowledge.

The second time of growth and change is during the caring and nurturing moments of congregational life. Worship, leadership education, nurture of adults, adolescents, and children, education for the ministries of the congregation, and care for shut-ins, sick, elderly, and bereaved are such experiences. We do not give sufficient critical thought to these activities. The *nature, quality, purposes, appropriateness,* and *timing* of these activities need to be continually examined. It is primarily through these activities, described in a traditional way, that we care for the health of the church. Our character shows most clearly in these program areas. Examination of these attributes in each of our programs will show us who we really are as a church.

Evaluation of these internal ministries of congregations

must take place constantly. We need to know if persons grow in their faith commitments through these ministries. Are persons equipped for the variety of ministries? Are we driving people away by the shabby quality, lack of direction, and unchristian character of our programs? Means of evaluation of the performance and function of each group in relation to the purposes and priorities of the whole body need to be a regular part of the life of each group and the whole organization. Energy and motivation for change come when we are faced with the truth about our performance. Our life needs to be characterized by our search for and encounter with the truth about ourselves, not by our avoidance of it.

The final time of transformation is during moments of support for persons and groups engaged in the ministries of the organization. We have not used our imagination in discovering ways to support one another as we are engaged in ministries both within and without local churches, judicatories, or boards and agencies. Church school teachers, many of whom are willing but not well equipped for their tasks, receive little support and encouragement from parents and the congregation. Laymen engaged in ministry within their secular work organizations find little understanding or support within the church for the tension, resistance, and opposition that meet their attempts to direct the resources of their companies toward problems of urban life. There is little caring for persons as they are involved in ministry with adolescents, or seek better education for the poor, or attempt to organize communities for more effective participation in decision-making.

Laymen's Sunday ought to be such an embarrassment

that we stop it. Every Sunday ought to be a time in which laymen who are engaged in the variety of ministries of the congregation can present their concerns and invite the congregation to participate in that ministry with them. Several congregations have "A Layman Speaks" regularly during Sunday morning worship services. Concerns about the ministry of the congregation to itself and the community are shared. Laymen are specifically invited to share their ministry and their concerns, not preach another sermon like the pastor.

In one of these congregations two months each year are set aside for focusing upon issues that are crucial to congregational life: worship, response to the racial crisis manifested in black power, education of the church, etc. Through total congregational involvement, understanding and support are developed for persons concerned about these issues in congregational life.

Congregations, judicatories, and boards and agencies must discover ways of supporting persons engaged in ministry. During periods of crisis, persons and organizations can grow if there is support. They can also disintegrate, retreat, and respond defensively if no support is available. Affirmation, understanding, development of economic and human resources, creation of structures to facilitate ministry, and ready access to the decision-making processes that affect these ministries are the most meaningful forms of support. When support is present during crisis, both persons and organizations can change.

It is not sufficient to encourage and enlist people for the ministries of the whole body. These persons are the body as they minister. The body must nourish and support the parts as they are doing the work of the body.

It is easiest to visualize the importance of support for ministries of local congregations. We need to recognize once again that judicatories, boards and agencies, and seminaries are parts of the body that need support if they are to function as members of the body. These groups in turn must support local congregations. The support from each of these groups need not be uncritical. It must be critical, if it is to be honest support, but there must be affirmation and understanding. There must be open, honest, and critical dialogue. No part can say to the other: "I have no need of you." There is too much domainism, protectionism, and defensiveness between parts of the same body. The end result is the sickness of the whole body and no one doing the work of the head, Jesus Christ. Living hope cannot emerge from a sick body.

Times of transformation are common to all church organizations. The need for growth is evident in every part. We have need of one another, for the healthiness that is in some parts to spread to other parts; for the faith resources in some members to revitalize others; for the work of the head that is clearly evident in some organs to become transplanted to others.

To write of the church in such crass, hard, and mundane ways may seem inappropriate and even unchristian. But it is in our most common practices—our procedures, functions, administrative practices, and educational programs—that we take most for granted, just where we have the possibility of most readily expressing our Christian faith and where we are already expressing some values and commitments. In this book we are encouraged to begin where we are, with our organizational life, and to attempt to discover what it means to be churchmen, persons who help the church to grow in its faith commitments and to express these in ordinary life.

Some may think this insufficient. It is! There are no ultimate human expressions of Christian faith, nor can we create such. But neither can we wait for the pillar of fire by day, a cloud by night, or the "zap" from above to bring some idealistic, utopian people of God. We can and are destroying one another while we wait.

We are a people for good or ill, faithful and unfaithful, who are called to be Christ's people in this strange, complex, organizational world. Our life, even if we do not like it, is composed of committees, task forces, endless meetings, minutes, people we do not agree with, and, always, a commission to get out into the world.

Hopeless? No! There is a source of hope in this organizational life of ours. We are called to subject it to the scrutiny of Christian faith and one another, and then work together to make our common life more just, more meaningful, more challenging, and more expressive of our common faith in Jesus of Nazareth.